Macmillan Computer Science Series

Consulting Editor: Professor F. H. Sumner, University of Manchester

A. Abdellatif, J. Le Bihan and M. Limame, *Oracle – A User's guide*
S.T. Allworth and R.N. Zobel, *Introduction to Real-time Software Design, second edition*
Ian O. Angell, *High-resolution Computer Graphics Using C*
Ian O. Angell and Gareth Griffith, *High-resolution Computer Graphics Using FORTRAN 77*
Ian O. Angell and Gareth Griffith, *High-resolution Computer Graphics Using Pascal*
M. Azmoodeh, *Abstract Data Types and Algorithms, second edition*
C. Bamford and P. Curran, *Data Structures, Files and Databases, second edition*
Philip Barker, *Author Languages for CAL*
R.E. Berry, B.A.E. Meekings and M.D. Soren, *A Book on C, second edition*
P. Beynon-Davies, *Information Systems Development*
G.M. Birtwistle, *Discrete Event Modelling on Simula*
B.G. Blundell, C.N. Daskalakis, N.A.E. Heyes and T.P. Hopkins, *An Introductory Guide to Silvar Lisco and HILO Simulators*
Richard Bornat, *Understanding and Writing Compilers*
Linda E.M. Brackenbury, *Design of VLSI Systems – A Practical Introduction*
Alan Bradley, *Peripherals for Computer Systems*
G.R. Brookes and A.J. Stewart, *Introduction to occam 2 on the Transputer*
J.K. Buckle, *Software Configuration Management*
W.D. Burnham and A.R. Hall, *Prolog Programming and Applications*
P.C. Capon and P.J. Jinks, *Compiler Engineering Using Pascal*
J.C. Cluley, *Introduction to Low Level Programming for Microprocessors*
Robert Cole, *Computer Communications, second edition*
E. Davalo and P. Naïm, *Neural Networks*
S.M. Deen, *Principles and Practice of Database Systems*
C. Delannoy, *Turbo Pascal Programming*
Tim Denvir, *Introduction to Discrete Mathematics for Software Engineering*
D. England *et al.*, *A Sun User's Guide*
J.S. Florentin, *Microprogrammed Systems Design*
A.B. Fontaine and F. Barrand, *80286 and 80386 Microprocessors*
J.B. Gosling, *Design of Arithmetic Units for Digital Computers*
M.G. Hartley, M. Healey and P.G. Depledge, *Mini and Microcomputer Systems*
J.A. Hewitt and R.J. Frank, *Software Engineering in Modula-2 – An Object-oriented Approach*
Roger Hutty, *COBOL 85 Programming*
Roland N. Ibbett and Nigel P. Topham, *Architecture of High Performance Computers, Volume I*
Roland N. Ibbett and Nigel P. Topham, *Architecture of High Performance Computers, Volume II*
Patrick Jaulent, *The 68000 – Hardware and Software*
P. Jaulent, L. Baticle and P. Pillot, *68020–30 Microprocessors and their Coprocessors*
M.J. King and J.P. Pardoe, *Program Design Using JSP – A Practical Introduction, second edition*
V.P. Lane, *Security of Computer Based Information Systems*
M. Léonard, *Database Design Theory*
David Lightfoot, *Formal Specification Using Z*
A.M. Lister and R.D. Eager, *Fundamentals of Operating Systems, fourth edition*

Continued overleaf

Macmillan Computer Science Series (continued)

Elizabeth Lynch, *Understanding SQL*
Tom Manns and Michael Coleman, *Software Quality Assurance*
R.J. Mitchell, *Microcomputer Systems Using the STE Bus*
R.J. Mitchell, *Modula-2 Applied*
Y. Nishinuma and R. Espesser, *UNIX – First Contact*
Pham Thu Quang and C. Chartier-Kastler, *MERISE in Practice*
A.J. Pilavakis, *UNIX Workshop*
E.J. Redfern, *Introduction to Pascal for Computational Mathematics*
Gordon Reece, *Microcomputer Modelling by Finite Differences*
F. D. Rolland, *Programming with VDM*
W.P. Salman, O. Tisserand and B. Toulout, *FORTH*
L.E. Scales, *Introduction to Non-Linear Optimization*
A.G. Sutcliffe, *Human–Computer Interface Design*
Colin J. Theaker and Graham R. Brookes, *Concepts of Operating Systems, second edition*
M. Thorin, *Real-time Transaction Processing*
M.R. Tolhurst *et al.*, *Open Systems Interconnection*
A.J. Tyrrell, *COBOL from Pascal*
M.J. Usher, *Information Theory for Information Technologists*
I.R. Wilson and A.M. Addyman, *A Practical Introduction to Pascal – with BS6192, second edition*

Non-series

Roy Anderson, *Management, Information Systems and Computers*
I.O. Angell, *Advanced Graphics with the IBM Personal Computer*
J.E. Bingham and G.W.P. Davies, *Planning for Data Communications*
B.V. Cordingley and D. Chamund, *Advanced BASIC Scientific Subroutines*
N. Frude, *A Guide to SPSS/PC+*
Percy Mett, *Introduction to Computing*
Tony Royce, *COBOL – An Introduction*
Tony Royce, *Structured COBOL – An Introduction*
Barry Thomas, *A PostScript Cookbook*

Formal Specification
Using Z

David Lightfoot

School of Computing and Mathematical Sciences
Oxford Brookes University

First published 1991 by
THE MACMILLAN PRESS LTD
Houndmills, Basingstoke, Hampshire RG21 2XS
and London
Companies and representatives
throughout the world

ISBN 0–333–54408–0

A catalogue record for this book is available
from the British Library.

Printed in China

Reprinted 1991, 1993

Contents

Preface

The aims of this book

This book aims to help readers learn about formal specification using the Z language. I believe that formal specification offers substantial benefits to the developers of computer systems and will make a major contribution towards improving their quality.

I further believe that if it is to make such contributions it must be used widely and not just by those with proven mathematical ability. Experience of teaching students who do not consider themselves mathematicians has convinced me that this is possible. Even if they do not use what they have learned immediately, the mathematical concepts of formal specification seem to help clarify thinking by providing a language for discussing the behaviour of computer systems.

The scope of this book

This book aims to cover the main ideas of formal specification in Z in a style which will be accessible to the reader who is not very familiar with mathematics. To achieve this the explanations have been kept somewhat informal, though I hope correct, and certain aspects of the notation have been given less emphasis than others or are even omitted.

How to use this book

The chapters of this book contain explanations of the mathematics of Z, interleaved with the development of an example specification. The chapters covering mathematics finish with a summary of the notation introduced in the chapter and a set of exercises. Sample solutions to selected exercises are included in an appendix.

The reader who is familiar with discrete mathematics may wish to concentrate on the chapters covering the examples and schemas, with only occasional reference to the tutorial chapters. On the other hand, the reader with little mathematical knowledge may wish to gain support from a book on discrete mathematics.

Acknowledgements

I am grateful to the members of the Programming Research Group of Oxford University, firstly for their pioneering work on Z and secondly for teaching it to me when I studied there for an MSc. What I have learned about Z is largely due to them, but I alone am responsible for any errors in this book.

I am also grateful for my then employer and colleagues for their assistance in making it possible for me to learn.

David Lightfoot, Oxford 1990

1   Introduction

The need for formal specification

Problems in the creation of computer systems

There are long-standing problems in the development of computer systems: often they take too much time to produce, cost more than estimated and fail to satisfy the customer. This "software crisis" was first identified in the nineteen-sixties and has been the subject of much research and controversy, and it is still not entirely solved.

Central to the problem is the fact that errors and inadequacies are more expensive to correct the later in the development process they are discovered. Furthermore, it is extremely difficult to clarify exactly what is required of a very complex system.

Software Engineering

A variety of techniques have been introduced to help deal with the difficulties of developing computer systems. These techniques are moving towards the concept of *software engineering*, where well established principles of the engineering professions are being applied to the creation of software systems. Amongst these principles is the idea that appropriate mathematical techniques should be applied in the analysis and solution of engineering problems.

Formal Methods

Techniques which use mathematical principles to develop computer systems are collectively known as *formal methods*. The idea of specifying what a computer system is required to do using a mathematical notation and techniques of mathematical manipulation, has led to notations for *formal specification*.

The role of mathematics

Background of mathematics

Mathematics has a very long history, spanning thousands of years of work by mathematicians in many different civilizations. The major principles of mathematics are now stable and proven in use in scientific and engineering applications. It is therefore appropriate to apply these to the development of computer systems.

Precision

Mathematical expressions have the advantage of being *precise*, because they rely only on a minimum of bases, and do not need any contextual information. All the information that is needed is formulated mathematically, and what is not needed is omitted.

Conciseness

Mathematical expressions are typically very concise; a great deal of meaning is concentrated in a relatively small number of symbols. This is a particular advantage when describing a very complex system.

Clarity

Mathematical forms are also *clear*, because of their independence from any cultural context, and because they are self contained. There is little scope for misunderstanding; a correct formulation can be easily seen to be correct and errors can be quickly identified.

Abstraction

The mathematical notion of *abstraction* plays an important role in formal methods. Abstraction involves initially considering only the essential issues of a problem and deferring consideration of all other aspects until a later stage. This *separation of concerns* is the best way of coping with the complexity of large systems.

Independence from natural language

The independence of mathematical forms from the context of spoken (natural) language means that mathematics can be equally well understood by all readers, irrespective of their language and culture.

Proofs

Deductions and conclusions expressed in a mathematical form are capable of being *proved*, by application of established mathematical laws. The ability to prove such things, rather than just to demonstrate them, or convince oneself informally of their validity, is an important aspect of the application of mathematics. This is particularly so when the consequences of an invalid conclusion could endanger life, in so-called *safety-critical* systems.

Current use of mathematics

Many practitioners involved with the development of computer systems are not mathematicians and do not make regular use of mathematics in their work. However, mathematical techniques are assuming an increasingly important role in the development of computer systems and it is appropriate that they should be known and applied by as many practitioners as possible.

Discrete mathematics

The mathematics used in formal specification is very simple. It is called *discrete mathematics* and is concerned more with sets and logic than with numbers. This means that even those who have studied mathematics before will probably have something new to learn. Conversely, those who have not previously been very successful at learning mathematics have a new area of mathematics to study and have the motivating factor that the benefits will be immediately applicable to their work.

In this book, all mathematical notations are introduced, with examples and, where necessary, a conventional or possible pronunciation is given. This can aid understanding and is also vital if people are to talk to each other about mathematics. However, the introductory mathematical parts are deliberately kept brief and in some places informal, since the topic of the book is the *application* of the mathematics. The reader who has need of further explanation, or more detailed mathematical justification, is encouraged to refer to a text on discrete mathematics. Titles of some of these can be found in the references section of this book.

Benefits and costs of formal specification

The benefits of formal specification are the benefits of using mathematics: formal specifications are precise, concise and clear and they help to separate different levels of abstraction. Deductions and conclusions drawn about systems being specified can be proved. Independence from natural language means that formal specification can be used by teams with members who speak different languages.

Some of the proofs used in formal specification are trivial and seem to amount to "proving the obvious". More significantly, others can be very complex and require mathematical skills which may be beyond the abilities of the normal user of formal specification. This book supplies the mathematical techniques from which proofs can be constructed but gives little emphasis to this aspect of formal specification. The reader interested in learning more about proofs and their benefits should refer to the references section of this book.

The use of *software tools* as an aid to proving is likely to grow in the near future.

The specification language Z

Background

The specification language Z (pronounced "zed" in Great Britain) was initiated by Jean-Raymond Abrial in France and developed by a team at the Programming Research Group (PRG) of Oxford University in England, led by Professor C.A.R. Hoare. It is foremost amongst specification notations in use at present, and its use is growing.

Z is used to specify new computer systems and to describe the behaviour of existing, complex computer systems.

Z is increasingly being learned by both practitioners of software engineering and by students. The aim of this book is to help in that process.

Software tools

The Z notation uses a set of characters some of which are not found on most typewriter or computer keyboards. Many of the extra characters are widely used mathematical symbols, but some are new and confined to Z.

In general, Z text cannot be prepared using conventional typewriting equipment and several *software tools* have been created to permit the typesetting of text written in Z. Some of these software tools also check the text to make sure that it conforms to the rules of the Z notation (its *syntax*).

Other software tools are concerned with giving automated assistance to the process of creating mathematical proofs. Some of these are called *theorem provers* and attempt the entire proof without manual intervention; others, called *proof assistants*, support the human activity of creating proofs.

Textual aspects of the Z notation

The Z notation is used in *specification documents* which consist of sections written in Z, interleaved with narrative text in natural language. Z also uses a graphical device called the *schema*, which is a box surrounding the mathematics. As well as having a useful effect in visually separating the mathematics from the narrative, schemas have important special properties which will be explained in this book.

Identifiers

There is a need to invent names when creating a formal specification. The rules for constructing such *identifiers* are similar to those of computer programming languages.

• Identifiers may be any length and are constructed from the (upper- and lower-case) Roman letters without diacritics, as used in English, and from the numeric digits.

• The first character must be a letter.

• The upper-case and lower-case letters are considered to be different. This is exploited in this book.

• Only a single word may be used for an identifier; when this needs to be
a compound of several words the *low-line* character (_) can be used, or the
convention of starting each component of the identifier with an upper-case
letter can be adopted. For example:

very_long_identifier
VeryLongIdentifier

The special characters Δ and Ξ on the front of an identifier, and ? and !
and ' on the end, have special meanings which will be explained later.

Stability of notation

The Z notation is relatively new and the need for standardization of
notation has only just arisen and has grown rapidly with the adoption of
software tools. Some of the notations used in this book will differ from
those in earlier texts. Sometimes the differences are small and cause no
misunderstandings. Occasionally there has been a major change in the
meaning of a symbol and in some instances this book mentions alternative
representations.

Handwritten form

Some of the symbols have a conventional handwritten form; the so-called
blackboard form, which differs slightly from the typeset form. In general,
it is advisable to copy the typeset form.

Exercises

1.1) An annual weekend event begins on the Friday evening and finishes
on the Sunday afternoon. The date of the event is specified as: "the last
weekend in September". What is the date of the Friday on which the event
begins if the last day of September (30th) in that year is:
   • a Monday
   • a Sunday
   • a Saturday
   • a Friday
Suggest an unambiguous specification of the date of the event.

1.2) On Friday the first of the month a software engineer goes away leaving an undated message on her/his desk saying: "Software engineer on leave until next Wednesday". A colleague from another department passes the desk on Monday 4th of the same month and reads the message. When would the colleague expect the software engineer next to be back at work?

1.3) A video cassette recorder has a "programming" facility which allows recordings to be made in the user's absence. Requests for recordings consist of: start-date, start-time, end-time and channel-number. Dates are specified by month-number and day-number. Times are given as hours and minutes using the 24-hour clock. If the end-time is earlier in the day than the start-time then the end-time is considered to be on the following day. Up to eight requests can be stored and are numbered one to eight.

How would you expect the recorder to behave in the following circumstances?

• start-date does not exist, for example, 31st April

• start-date does not exist; not a leap year, 29 February

• start- and end-times for different requests overlap (on same day)

• start-date is for New Year's Eve and end-time is earlier in the day than start-time.

• requests are not in chronological order. For example, request 1 is for a recording which occurs later than that of request 2.

Look at the user handbook for a video cassette recorder similar to the one described here. Does the handbook answer these questions?

1.4) In the requirements specification of a computer program it is stated that: "The records input to the program should be sorted in order of increasing key."

Does this mean that the program may be written on the assumption that the records will already have been sorted (by some external agent), or does it mean that the program must perform the required sorting?

1.5) Look at the manual(s) for any reasonably complex machine or system. Find the parts which are ambiguous or unclear and pose questions that are reasonable to ask but which are not answered by the manual.

2   Sets in Z

Types

A *set* is a collection of values called *elements* or *members*. The Z notation also uses the notion of *type*; all the possible values of a set are considered to have something in common, and are said to have the same type. Any set is therefore considered to be a *subset* of its type.

The notion of type helps in two ways:

- It avoids certain mathematical paradoxes

- It allows checks to be made that statements about sets make sense.

The checks can be automated by means of computer *software tools* which check the consistency of the mathematical text in a Z document in the same sort of way that a spelling checker checks the consistency of a document in a natural language.

The need to determine the type of all values used in a Z specification is not really a disadvantage since the types used are either *built-in* types, *free* types or *basic* types.

Built-in types

Integer

Built-in types can be used in any Z document without the need to introduce them explicitly. The Z notation has only one built-in type, *integer*:

$$\mathbb{Z} = ..., -3, -2, -1, 0, 1, 2, 3, ...$$

This type is sometimes written "ZZ" and pronounced "zed-zed". It is an example of an *infinite* set.

Natural

A widely used set is the set of *natural* numbers, which in Z consists of the *non-negative* integers:

N = 0, 1, 2, 3, ...

Although it is often used to declare variables, this set (pronounced "natural" or "en-en") is not considered to be a *type* in Z. It is a *subset* of its underlying type, which is integer.

In some mathematical contexts the natural numbers are not considered to include zero. The set of natural numbers excluding zero can be written as follows in Z:

N_1

Operations on integers

The following operators are defined for the type integer and its subsets:

+	addition
−	subtraction
*	multiplication
÷	(integer) division
mod	modulus (remainder after division)

The normal rules of precedence between operators hold. For example:

$23 \div 5 = 4$
$23 \bmod 5 = 3$

Others

The Z notation does not include the set of *real* (fractional) numbers as a built-in type. In a specification which needs real numbers one could define the type *REAL* and regard integer as a *set*, a *subset* of the type REAL.

Furthermore Z does not include the set of *characters* as a built-in type. If needed it could be introduced as a *basic* type, or as a *free* type, in which case its values would be enumerated. The identifiers of types are conventionally made entirely of capital letters.

Basic types

Basic types are also called *given sets*. The basic types of a specification are declared without concern for what their actual elements are. For example a specification might refer to the set of all possible car registrations, without considering how such registrations are represented as characters. A basic type is declared by writing its name in square brackets, with a comment to indicate its intended meaning. The set of car registrations might be called REGISTRATION and written:

[REGISTRATION]   the set of all possible car registrations

By convention, the name of a basic type is written entirely in capital letters and a singular noun is used.

Another basic type might be the set of all drivers:

[DRIVER]   the set of all legal drivers

Several types can be given in one line:

[REGISTRATION, DRIVER]

In general, basic types should be chosen to be as widely encompassing as possible. Furthermore it should be assumed that the elements of the type are uniquely identifiable. For example, if it is necessary to consider people, the basic type used might be:

[PERSON]   the set of all, uniquely identifiable persons

This disregards the fact that several people can have the same name; that is a separate issue.

Free types

Sometimes it is convenient to introduce a type by enumerating the identifiers of each of its elements. This can be done with a *free type*. The general format is:

freeType ::= element$_1$ | element$_2$ | ... | element$_n$

Examples are:

RESPONSE ::= yes | no
STATUS ::= inUse | free | onHold | outOfOrder

Declarations

One of the requirements of typed set theory is that all names designating values be *declared*, that is their type must be stated. For example to introduce a named value *chauffeur* to be of the basic type *DRIVER* one must write:

chauffeur: DRIVER

This can be pronounced, "*chauffeur* is one of the set of values *DRIVER*" or "*chauffeur* is drawn from the set *DRIVER*" or "*chauffeur* is a *DRIVER*".

In the following examples elements will be drawn from the set *EC*, the set of all countries in the European Community. This set is used for the sake of illustration since it (currently) contains only twelve members, which will be identified for the brevity's sake, by their international car registration letters:

• Belgium	B	• Great Britain	GB
• Netherlands	NL	• Italy	I
• Luxembourg	L	• Ireland	IRL
• France	F	• Germany	D
• Denmark	DK	• Spain	E
• Portugal	P	• Greece	GR

EC ::= B | NL | L | F | DK | P | GB | I | IRL | D | E | GR
the set of countries currently in the European Community

Single value from a type

To introduce a *variable* called *homeland* to refer to one country in the European Community one would write:

homeland: EC

A value can be given to *homeland* by writing:

> homeland = GB

Sets of values

When a name is to be given to a *set* of values, the name is declared as being a *powerset* of the type of the elements:

> benelux: ℙEC

This can be read "*benelux* is a subset of the set of countries *EC*", or "*benelux* is set of *EC* countries".

(Benelux is a name sometimes used for the group of countries consisting of Belgium, the Netherlands and Luxembourg.)

Powersets will be considered in a later section of this chapter.

Set constants

A set of values is written by enumerating the set's values within braces:

> benelux = {B, NL, L}

Order does not matter:

> {B, NL, L} = {NL, B, L} = { L, B, NL} =
> {B, L, NL} = {NL, L, B} = {L, NL, B}

Repeating a term does not matter; it can only be in a set once:

> {B, NL, L, NL} = {B, NL, L}

The empty set

It is possible to have a set with no values; it is called the empty set:

> Ø

The empty set is also written as empty braces:

{ }

A set which contains only one elements is called a *singleton* set.

{GB}

Note that a set containing a single element has different type from the element itself: GB does not have the same type as {GB}.

Operators

Equivalence

Two values of the same type can be tested to see if they are the same by using the equals sign, as in

$x = y$

Two sets are equal if they contain exactly the same elements.

Non-equivalence

Similarly, two values of the same type can be tested to see if they are *not* the same by using the not-equals sign, as in

$x \neq y$

Two sets are not-equal if they do not contain exactly the same elements.

Numerical relations

The following relational operators are applicable to integers:

<	less than
≤	less than or equal to
>	greater than
≥	greater than or equal to

Membership

The *membership* operator is written

∈

and is pronounced "is an element of" or "is a member of". The expression involving it is true if the value is an element (member) of the set and otherwise false:

NL ∈ {B, NL, L}   this is true

The diagrams in this chapter used to illustrate the set operators are called *Venn* diagrams.

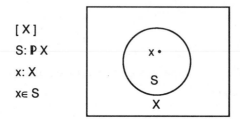

Figure 2.1

The *non-membership* operator is written

∉

and is pronounced "is not an element of" or "is not a member of". The expression involving it is true if the value is *not* an element (member) of the set and otherwise false:

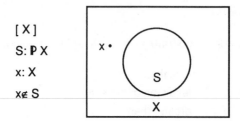

Figure 2.2

GB ∉ {B, NL, L}   this is true

Note that the value to be tested for membership must be an element of the underlying type of the set. The expression:

USA ∈ {B, NL, L}

is neither true nor false but *illegal*, since *USA* is not an element of the type *EC*.

Size, cardinality

The number of values in a set is called its *size* or *cardinality* and is signified by the *hash* sign, acting as a function:

# {B, NL, L}	= 3
# {GB}	= 1
# GB	illegal, GB is not a set
# Ø	= 0

Powersets

The *powerset* of a set *S*, is written

$$\mathbb{P}S$$

and is the set of all its subsets. For example:

$\mathbb{P}$ {B, NL, L} =	
{ Ø,	the empty set
{B}, {NL}, {L},	all the singletons
{B, NL}, {B, L}, {NL, L},	all the pairs
{B, NL, L}}	all three elements

Note that the size of the powerset is two raised to the power of the size of the set:

# ($\mathbb{P}$S)	$= 2^{\#S}$ (for any set S)
# {B, NL, L}	= 3
# ($\mathbb{P}$ {B, NL, L})	= 8

Finite sets

Although some of the sets used in Z specifications are infinite, such as the natural numbers, most are finite. If necessary one can indicate that a subset is finite by using the symbol

$$\mathbb{F}$$

for finite powerset. Occasionally

  F$_1$

is used to indicate the subset with at most one element. This can be used to
indicate that the element may be present or absent.

Set inclusion

The operator

  $\subseteq$

is pronounced "is included in" or "is contained in" and tests whether the
first set is included in the second set; whether the first is a subset of the
second:

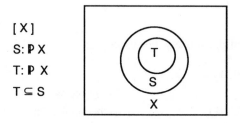

$$[\,X\,]$$
$$S: \mathbb{P}\,X$$
$$T: \mathbb{P}\,X$$
$$T \subseteq S$$

Figure 2.3

{B, NL} $\subseteq$ {B, NL, L}	this is true
$\varnothing \subseteq$ {B, NL, L}	this is true
{B, NL, L} $\subseteq$ {B, NL, L}	this is true

  The empty set is included in all sets.

Strict inclusion

The operator

  $\subset$

denotes *strict inclusion*; the first set may not be *equal to* the second

{B, NL, L} ⊆ {B, NL, L}   this is true
{B, NL, L} ⊂ {B, NL, L}   this is false
S ⊂ T   is the same as S ⊆ T AND S ≠ T

Union

The *union* of two sets is the set containing all the elements that are in either the first set or the second set or both:

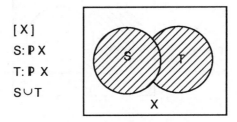

Figure 2.4

{B, D, DK} ∪ {D, DK, F, I} = {B, D, DK, F, I}
{B, D, DK} ∪ {DK, F, I} = {B, D, DK, F, I}
{B, NL, L} ∪ {GB, IRL} = {B, NL, L, GB, IRL}
{B, D, DK} ∪ ∅ = {B, D, DK}

Intersection

The *intersection* of two sets is the set containing all the elements that are in both the first set and the second set:

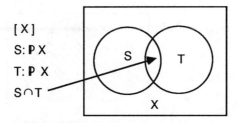

Figure 2.5

{B, D, DK} ∩ {D, DK, F, I} = {D, DK}
{B, D, DK} ∩ {DK, F, I} = {DK}
{B, D, DK} ∩ ∅ = ∅

Difference

The *difference* of two sets is the set containing all those elements of the first set that are *not* in the second set:

$$\{B, D, DK, F, I\} \setminus \{B, D, GR\} = \{DK, F, I\}$$
$$\{B, D, DK\} \setminus \emptyset = \{B, D, DK\}$$

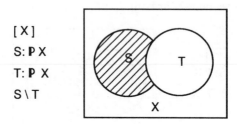

[X]

S: $\mathbb{P}$ X

T: $\mathbb{P}$ X

S \ T

Figure 2.6

Distributed union

The operations described so far have been applied to *two* sets. Sometimes it is useful to be able to refer to the union of several sets; in fact, of a *set* of sets. This can be done with the *distributed union* operator, written as an oversize union operator sign, which applies to a set of sets and results in a set:

$$\bigcup \{\{B, N, L\}, \{F, D, L, I\}, \{GB, GR, B, IRL, DK, E, P\}\}$$
$$= \{B, N, L, F, D, I, GB, GR, IRL, DK, E, P\}$$

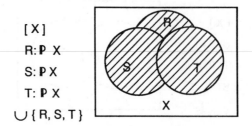

[X]

R: $\mathbb{P}$ X

S: $\mathbb{P}$ X

T: $\mathbb{P}$ X

$\bigcup \{ R, S, T \}$

Figure 2.7

The distributed union of a set of sets is those elements which occur in at least one of the component sets.

Distributed intersection

The *distributed intersection* of a set of sets is the set of elements which are in all of the component sets:

$$\cap \{ \{B, N, L, DK\}, \{F, L, DK, D, I\}, \{GB, DK, L, E, P\} \} = \{DK, L\}$$

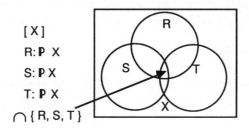

Figure 2.8

Set comprehension

The constructors for sets so far introduced have required that all the elements be enumerated. It is also possible to construct a set by giving a condition (a *predicate*) which must hold for all members of the set. This can be done by a form called a *set comprehension* and the general form is:

{declaration | constraint • expression}

For example:

{x: **N** | even(x) • x}   the even natural numbers
{x: **N** | even(x) • x * x} the squares of the even natural numbers
{country: EC | neutral(country) • country}   the neutral EC countries

The constraint and its preceding bar may be omitted:

{x: **N** • x * x}   the squares of the natural numbers

Ranges of numbers

The range of values

m .. n

stands for the numbers m to n inclusive

$$\{\, i: \mathbb{Z} \mid m \le i \text{ AND } i \le n \bullet i \,\}$$

Disjoint sets

Sets which are *disjoint* have no elements in common; their intersection is the empty set. This is easily expressed for two sets S and T

$$S \cap T = \varnothing$$

For more than two sets it become more lengthy since every *pair* of sets must have empty intersections. For example for sets A, B and C to be disjoint:

$$A \cap B = \varnothing$$
$$B \cap C = \varnothing$$
$$A \cap C = \varnothing$$

In general one can write:

disjoint $\langle S, T \rangle$
disjoint $\langle A, B, C \rangle$

[HUMAN]
female, male: $\mathbb{P}$ HUMAN

disjoint $\langle$ female, male $\rangle$

The brackets here are *sequence brackets* which will be explained later.

Partition

A *sequence* of sets is said to *partition* another larger set if the sets are disjoint and their distributed union is the entire large set. For example, the sets A, B and C partition T if:

disjoint $\langle A, B, C \rangle$

and

$$\bigcup \{ A, B, C \} = T$$

This can be written:

⟨A, B, C⟩ partition T

For example:

⟨female, male⟩ partition HUMAN

Summary of notation

Z	the set of integers (whole numbers)
N	the set of natural numbers (≥ 0)
N$_1$	the set of positive natural numbers (≥ 1)
$t \in S$	t is an element of S
$t \notin S$	t is not an element of S
$S \subseteq T$	S is contained in T.
$S \subset T$	S is strictly contained in T. ($S \neq T$)
$\emptyset$ or { }	the empty set
$\{t_1, t_2, \ldots t_n\}$	the set containing $t_1, t_2, \ldots t_n$
ℙS	Powerset: the set of all subsets of S
𝔽S	the set of finite subsets of S
$S \cup T$	Union: elements that are either in S or T
$S \cap T$	Intersection: elements that are both in S and in T
$S \setminus T$	Difference: elements that are in S but not in T
#S	Size: number of elements in S
{D | P • t}	the set of t's such that given the declarations D, P holds
m .. n	the set of numbers m to n inclusive
$\bigcup$SS	the distributed union of the set of sets SS
$\bigcap$SS	the distributed intersection of the set of sets SS
disjoint sqs	the sets in the sequence sqs are disjoint
sqs partition S	the sets in sqs partition the set S

Exercises

2.1) Certain people are registered as users of a computer system. At any given time, some of these users are "logged-in" to the computer. (There is no multiple log-in; a user is either logged-in or not.)

Describe this situation using the concepts of Z covered so far.

2.2 Extend your description from question 2.1 as follows:
• There is a limit (between 32 and 128) to the number of users logged-in at any time.

2.3) Extend your description from question 2.1 as follows:
• There are two groups of users: staff and customers.

2.4) Express the following statements using Z notations:
• all the currrently logged-in users are staff
• there are more customer users than staff users.

2.5) Is the following expression true?

#loggedIn ≤ # users

3   Using sets to describe a system – a simple example

Introduction

With only the mathematics covered so far it is possible to describe a very simple computer system. More realistic systems will need more theory, which will be covered later.

This example concerns recording the passengers aboard an aircraft. There are no seat numbers, passengers are allowed aboard on a first-come-first-served basis, and the aircraft has a fixed capacity.

The only *basic type* involved here is the set of all possible persons, called *PERSON*.

> [PERSON]   the set of all possible uniquely identified persons

Normally people are identified by name and the possibility of two or more persons having the same name poses difficulties. For this example people are assumed to be identified *uniquely*; for example, by identity-card number or passport number.

The capacity of the aircraft is a natural number called *capacity*. Its actual value is not relevant to the specification; it could even be zero:

> capacity: N   the seating capacity of the aircraft

The state

The state of the system is given by the set of people on board the aircraft. This can be described by a set of persons, *onboard*, one of the many subsets of the set *PERSON*:

onboard: ℙPERSON

The number of persons on board must never exceed the capacity:

#onboard ≤ capacity

This is an *invariant* property of all states of the system. No operation will be permitted to lead the system into a state for which it does not hold. Finding the invariant properties which exist between components of a system is a very important early stage of formal specification.

Initial state

There must be an initial state for the system. The obvious one is where the aircraft is empty:

onboard = Ø

The initial state must satisfy the invariant property. This it clearly does, since the size of the empty set is zero, which is less than or equal to all natural numbers and so to all possible values of *capacity*.

Operations

Boarding

There must be an operation to allow a person, *p*, to board the aircraft. This changes the value of *onboard*. The value of *onboard* after an operation is denoted by *onboard'* (pronounced "onboard prime"):

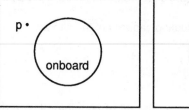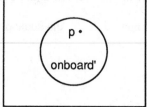

Figure 3.1

onboard' = onboard ∪ {p}

Note that *{p}* is the singleton set containing just the value *p*.

Precondition of boarding

Each normal boarding operation increases the size of the set *onboard* by one, so eventually the size of *onboard* would exceed *capacity*, thus violating the invariant condition. Therefore it is a necessary precondition of this operation that the size of *onboard* is strictly less than *capacity*:

    #onboard < capacity

It would clearly be an error to record the boarding of a person who is already recorded as being on board, so a further precondition is:

    p ∉ onboard

To summarize:

    p: PERSON

    p ∉ onboard
    #onboard < capacity
    onboard' = onboard ∪ {p}

Decisions regarding the behaviour of the system when the preconditions are not satisfied are best deferred. The Z language offers a convenient notation for adding to a specification at a later stage.

Disembark

It is also necessary to have an operation to allow a person to disembark from the aircraft. The effect on *onboard* is:

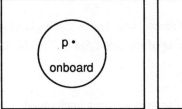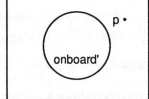

Figure 3.2

onboard' = onboard \ {p}

The precondition of this operation is that the person *p* be aboard

p ∈ onboard

To summarize:

p: PERSON

p ∈ onboard
onboard' = onboard \ {p}

Enquiry operations

Number on board

In addition to operations which change the state of the system it is necessary to have an operation to discover the number of persons on board: *numonboard*. This has no precondition; it always works. It leaves the value of *onboard* unchanged:

numonboard: **N**

numonboard = #onboard
onboard' = onboard

Note that it is necessary to state *explicitly* that *onboard* does not change. To say nothing about *onboard'* would imply that it could have *any* value after the operation.

Person on board

Finally, a useful enquiry is to discover whether or not a given person *p* is on board. The reply will be a value of the free type *RESPONSE*, declared:

RESPONSE ::= yes | no

There is no precondition and the state remains unchanged:

p: PERSON
reply: RESPONSE

```
((p ∈ onboard AND reply = "yes")
OR
(p ∉ onboard AND reply = "no"))

onboard' = onboard
```

The logical operators *AND* and *OR* will be covered in a later chapter. This section can be read: "either *p* is onboard and the reply is *yes* or *p* is not onboard and the reply is *no*. The state is unchanged."

Conclusion

Although the system described here is very simple, it has been described using the concepts of set theory. The description is not complete since treatment of violation of preconditions has been deferred, but the description will be augmented later. The purpose of this example has been to give a first taste of the use of mathematics to describe a system.

Exercises

For a computer system as described in question 2.1:

3.1) Discover any invariant properties.

3.2) Define a suitable initial state for this system.

3.3) Define an operation to register a person as a new user, who is not initially logged-in.

3.4) Define an operation to remove a user's registration, when the user is not logged-in.

3.5) Define operations for a user to log in and to log out.
   In each case explain your formulations in narrative text.

4   Logic: propositional calculus

Introduction

The example at the end of the previous chapter which discovered whether or not a person was on board an aircraft used the *logical operators AND* and *OR*. This chapter gives a fuller explanation of these and other logical operators.

Propositional calculus

Propositional calculus is also known as *Boolean algebra* and is named after the mathematician George Boole. It is concerned with statements, called *propositions*, which may be either true or false. The values that the propositions may take are denoted by the words *true* and *false* in Z but the following alternatives are sometimes used in other contexts:

true	TRUE	T	1
false	FALSE	F	0

Operators

Since there are only two possible values that a proposition can take it is practical to explain the action of operators by enumerating all results. This is done using a table called a *truth table*. The following operators can be applied to propositions:

Negation

The *negation* operator is pronounced "not" and is written:

but the following are also used:

NOT   ~   ⎯ (written on top of the proposition)

For any proposition P, the truth table for negation is:

P	$\neg P$
false	true
true	false

When P is *false*, $\neg P$ is *true*; when P is *true*, $\neg P$ is *false*.

Conjunction

The *conjunction* operator is pronounced "and" and is written:

$\wedge$

but the following are also used:

AND   &   .

(To remember this symbol: $\wedge$ looks like the A of AND.)

Given propositions P and Q, the truth table for conjunction is:

P	Q	$P \wedge Q$
false	false	false
false	true	false
true	false	false
true	true	true

The proposition $P \wedge Q$ is true only when both P is *true* and Q is *true*, otherwise it is *false*.

Disjunction

The *disjunction* operator is pronounced "or" and is written:

$\vee$

but the following are also used:

OR   +

Given propositions P and Q, the truth table for disjunction is:

P	Q	$P \vee Q$
false	false	false
false	true	true
true	false	true
true	true	true

The proposition $P \vee Q$ is *true* only when either P is *true* or Q is *true* or both are *true*. It is *false* when both P and Q are *false*.

Implication

The *implication* operator is pronounced "implies" or "if ...then" as in "P implies Q" or "if P then Q" and is written:

$\Rightarrow$

Given propositions P and Q, the truth table for implication is:

P	Q	$P \Rightarrow Q$
false	false	true
false	true	true
true	false	false
true	true	true

The proposition $P \Rightarrow Q$ is *false* only when P is *true* and Q is *false*. A useful relationship between implication and disjunction is

$P \Rightarrow Q$ is equivalent to $\neg P \vee Q$

This is useful for removing implications when manipulating expressions.

Equivalence

The *equivalence* operator is pronounced "is equivalent to" or "if and only if" and is written:

⇔

Given propositions P and Q, the truth table for equivalence is:

P	Q	$P \Leftrightarrow Q$
false	false	true
false	true	false
true	false	false
true	true	true

The proposition $P \Leftrightarrow Q$ is *true* only when P is the same as Q.
The equivalence given above for implication can be written:

$$P \Rightarrow Q \Leftrightarrow \neg P \vee Q$$

A useful law relating implication to equivalence is:

$$(P \Rightarrow Q) \wedge (Q \Rightarrow P) \Leftrightarrow (P \Leftrightarrow Q)$$

De Morgan's laws

The following important laws relating negation, conjunction and disjunction are due to the mathematician Augustus de Morgan

$$\neg(P \wedge Q) \Leftrightarrow \neg P \vee \neg Q$$
$$\neg(P \vee Q) \Leftrightarrow \neg P \wedge \neg Q$$

These are useful for removing brackets when manipulating expressions.

Demonstrating laws

A *law* is a relationship which holds good irrespective of the actual values of the propositions involved. Truth tables can be used to demonstrate the validity of a law. For example, to show the validity of the first of de Morgan's laws given above:

$$\neg(P \wedge Q) \Leftrightarrow \neg P \vee \neg Q$$

P	Q	P ∧ Q	¬ (P ∧ Q)
false	false	false	true
false	true	false	true
true	false	false	true
true	true	true	false

¬ P	¬ Q	¬ P ∨ ¬ Q	¬(P ∧ Q) ⇔ ¬P ∨ ¬Q
true	true	true	true
true	false	true	true
false	true	true	true
false	false	false	true

Using laws

Laws are used to prove that two statements in the propositional calculus, which are not necessarily identical, are equivalent. In formal specification laws are used in chains of transformations called *proofs* which can verify that a specification is consistent and make deductions about the behaviour of a system from its specification.

Example proof – exclusive-or

The *exclusive-or* operator (often written *xor*) is sometimes needed to relate two propositions. It gives true if one or other proposition is true but not both. (The disjunction operator is an *inclusive* or.) It is not a basic operator of propositional calculus but it can be formulated from the existing operators in (at least) two ways:

$$P \text{ xor } Q \Leftrightarrow (P \lor Q) \land \lnot(P \land Q)$$
$$P \text{ xor } Q \Leftrightarrow (P \land \lnot Q) \lor (\lnot P \land Q)$$

These could be shown to be equivalent by means of a truth table, but a proof by application of laws taken from the list which follows is also possible and such a proof is more practical in cases where more than two propositions are involved.

The proof which follows is deliberately made very laborious so that every transformation will be visible and justified. In practice many simple transformations are made from one line to the next and simple laws such as commutativity are not cited.

In general deriving proofs is a mathematical skill which must be learned and which is beyond the scope of this book. Software tools are now available to assist in the derivation of proofs.

$(P \vee Q) \wedge \neg(P \wedge Q)$ first formulation

$\Leftrightarrow$

$(P \vee Q) \wedge (\neg P \vee \neg Q)$ by de Morgan's *and*

$\Leftrightarrow$

$((P \vee Q) \wedge \neg P)$
$\vee ((P \vee Q) \wedge \neg Q)$ by distribution of *or* over *and*

$\Leftrightarrow$

$(\neg P \wedge (P \vee Q))$
$\vee (\neg Q \wedge (P \vee Q))$ by commutativity of *and* (twice)

$\Leftrightarrow$

$((\neg P \wedge P) \vee (\neg P \wedge Q))$
$\vee ((\neg Q \wedge P) \vee (\neg Q \wedge Q))$ by distribution of *or* over *and*

$\Leftrightarrow$

$((P \wedge \neg P) \vee (\neg P \wedge Q))$
$\vee ((\neg Q \wedge P) \vee (Q \wedge \neg Q))$ commutative *and* (twice)

$\Leftrightarrow$

$(false \vee (\neg P \wedge Q))$
$\vee ((\neg Q \wedge P) \vee false)$ by contradiction (twice)

$\Leftrightarrow$

$((\neg P \wedge Q) \vee false)$
$\vee ((\neg Q \wedge P) \vee false)$ by commutativity of *or*

$\Leftrightarrow$

$(\neg P \wedge Q)$
$\vee (\neg Q \wedge P)$ by *or* simplification 3 (twice)

$\Leftrightarrow$

$(\neg P \wedge Q)$

$\vee (P \wedge \neg Q)$ by commutativity of *and*

$\Leftrightarrow$

$(P \wedge \neg Q) \vee (\neg P \wedge Q)$ by commutativity of *or*

Laws about logical operators

Given propositions *P*, *Q* and *R*:

Law	Name
$(P \wedge Q) \Leftrightarrow (Q \wedge P)$	commutativity of *and*
$(P \vee Q) \Leftrightarrow (Q \vee P)$	commutativity of *or*
$(P \Leftrightarrow Q) \Leftrightarrow (Q \Leftrightarrow P)$	commutativity of *equivalence*

$P \wedge (Q \wedge R) \Leftrightarrow (P \wedge Q) \wedge R$

$\quad\quad\quad\quad\quad \Leftrightarrow P \wedge Q \wedge R$ associativity of *and*

$P \vee (Q \vee R) \Leftrightarrow (P \vee Q) \vee R$

$\quad\quad\quad\quad\quad \Leftrightarrow P \vee Q \vee R$ associativity of *or*

Law	Name
$P \wedge (Q \vee R) \Leftrightarrow (P \wedge Q) \vee (P \wedge R)$	distribution of *or* over *and*
$P \vee (Q \wedge R) \Leftrightarrow (P \vee Q) \wedge (P \vee R)$	distribution of *and* over *or*
$\neg(P \wedge Q) \Leftrightarrow \neg P \vee \neg Q$	de Morgan's *and*
$\neg(P \vee Q) \Leftrightarrow \neg P \wedge \neg Q$	de Morgan's *or*
$\neg(\neg P) \Leftrightarrow P$	negation
$P \vee \neg P \Leftrightarrow true$	excluded middle
$P \wedge \neg P \Leftrightarrow false$	contradiction
$P \Rightarrow Q \Leftrightarrow \neg P \vee Q$	implication
$(P \Leftrightarrow Q) \Leftrightarrow (P \Rightarrow Q) \wedge (Q \Rightarrow P)$	equality

P ∨ P ⇔ P	*or* simplification 1
P ∨ true ⇔ true	*or* simplification 2
P ∨ false ⇔ P	*or* simplification 3
P ∨ (P ∧ Q) ⇔ P	*or* simplification 4

P ∧ P ⇔ P	*and* simplification 1
P ∧ true ⇔ P	*and* simplification 2
P ∧ false ⇔ false	*and* simplification 3
P ∧ (P ∨ Q) ⇔ P	*and* simplification 4

Priorities (highest to lowest)

¬

∧

∨

⇒

⇔

Relationship between logic and set theory

There is a direct relationship between some of the operators of logic and operations on sets and logical operations are sometimes illustrated by Venn diagrams.

In the following explanations, the symbol

==

signifies an *abbreviation definition*. In general

A == B

means "*A* is an abbreviated way of writing *B*".

[X]	any set

S, T: ℙX

S ∪ T == {x: X | x ∈ S ∨ x ∈ T • x}

S ∩ T == {x: X | x ∈ S ∧ x ∈ T • x}

S \ T == {x: X | x ∈ S ∧ x ∉ T • x}

Summary of notation

true, false	logical constants
$\neg\, P$	negation: "not P"
$P \wedge Q$	conjunction: "P and Q"
$P \vee Q$	disjunction: "P or Q"
$P \Rightarrow Q$	implication: "P implies Q" or "if P then Q"
$P \Leftrightarrow Q$	equivalence: "P is logically equivalent to Q"
$t1 = t2$	equality between terms
$t_1 \neq t_2$	$\neg(t_1 = t_2)$

Exercises

4.1) Show by truth table that:

$$(P \Rightarrow Q) \Leftrightarrow (\neg\, P \vee Q)$$

4.2) Show by truth table that:

$$((P \Rightarrow Q) \wedge (Q \Rightarrow P)) \Leftrightarrow (P \Leftrightarrow Q)$$

4.3) By using laws from this chapter simplify:

$$\neg(p \notin onboard \wedge \#onboard < capacity)$$

4.4) By using laws from this chapter simplify:

$$(a \wedge b) \vee (a \wedge c) \vee (a \wedge \neg\, c)$$

4.5) Given

$$p \in loggedIn \Rightarrow p \in user$$

convince yourself that

$$p \in loggedIn \wedge p \in user$$

can be simplified to

$$p \in loggedIn$$

5   The example extended

Full definition of boarding operation

The definitions of the operations for boarding and disembarking from the aircraft in the example of the Chapter Three did not consider what was to happen if the precondition of an operation was not fulfilled. Now this will be rectified. Each operation will have an additional observation, *reply*, which gives a response to indicate what happened during the operation. The response will be a value of the type *RESPONSE*:

> RESPONSE ::= OK | onBoard | full | notOnBoard | twoErrors

Board

The operation to board the aircraft can now be given:

> p: PERSON
> reply: RESPONSE
>
> (p ∉ onboard ∧ #onboard < capacity ∧
> onboard' = onboard ∪ {p} ∧ reply = OK)
> ∨
> (p ∈ onboard ∧ #onboard = capacity
> ∧ onboard' = onboard ∧ reply = twoErrors)
> ∨
> (p ∈ onboard ∧ #onboard < capacity ∧
> onboard' = onboard ∧ reply = onBoard)
> ∨
> (p ∉ onboard ∧ #onboard = capacity ∧
> onboard' = onboard ∧ reply = full)

37

Disembark

The operation to disembark from the aircraft can now be given:

```
p: PERSON
reply: RESPONSE


(p ∈ onboard ∧
onboard' = onboard \ {p} ∧ reply = OK)

∨

(p ∉ onboard ∧
onboard' = onboard ∧ reply = notOnBoard)
```

Note this is simpler than the operation *Board* since if the number on board is zero

```
#onboard = 0
```

p cannot be a member of *onboard*, so there is no need to test explicitly for *p* on board.

A better way

As can be seen, this way of defining the operations in full begins to get complicated. A much better, *modular*, approach using *schemas* will be introduced next.

Exercises

Referring to exercise 2.1 and its development in exercises of Chapter 3, give full descriptions, in the manner of this chapter, for:

5.1) a type for the response from any of the following operations.

5.2) the operation to register a new user.

5.3) the operation to remove a user's registration.

5.4) the operation to log in.

5.5) the operation to log out.

6   Schemas

Schemas

A specification document in Z consists of narrative text written in a natural language such as English, interspersed with formal descriptions written in the Z notation. As a way of making a clear separation between these two components a graphical format called the *schema* (plural *schemas*) was devised. The schema form also has various useful mathematical properties.

Here is an example of a schema:

$$
\begin{array}{|l}
\hline
S \\\\
\hline
a, b: \quad \mathbb{N} \\\\
\hline
a < b \\\\
\hline
\end{array}
$$

The schema is called S and it declares (introduces) two *observations* (also called *variables*) a and b. It also contains a constraining *predicate* which states that a must be less than b.

The horizontal lines of the schema normally extend far enough to the right to reach the longest line of the declarations or of the predicate.

A schema can also be written in an equivalent *linear* form, which is sometimes more convenient:

$$S \triangleq [\, a, b: \mathbb{N} \mid a < b \,]$$

The operator

$$\triangleq$$

means "stands for" and indicates textual equivalence.

The general form of a schema is:

$$\begin{array}{|l}
\underline{\text{SchemaName}} \\
\text{declarations} \\
\hline
\text{predicate} \\
\hline
\end{array}$$

and the form of the linear schema is

$$\text{SchemaName} \triangleq [\ \text{declarations} \mid \text{predicate}\ ]$$

It is possible to have an *anonymous* schema, in which case the schema name would be omitted. Furthermore it is possible to have a schema with no predicate part. In this case the schema would simply declare a new observation or observations without applying a constraining predicate.

An observation introduced by a schema is *local* to that schema and may only be referenced in another schema by explicitly *including* the observation's defining schema. This is sometimes inconvenient and it is also possible to introduce observations which are available throughout the specification. These are known as *global* observations and are introduced by an *axiomatic* definition.

For example, the capacity of an aircraft is introduced as a global observation by:

$$\text{capacity:}\qquad \mathbb{N}$$

If you wish to add a constraining predicate to the observation you can use the general form:

$$\begin{array}{|l}
\text{declarations} \\
\hline
\text{predicate} \\
\end{array}$$

For example, to introduce a limit to the number of participants who may enrol on a course, *maxOnCourse*, where this limit must be in the range six to 30, you could use the following:

$$\begin{array}{|l}
\text{maxOnCourse:}\qquad \mathbb{N} \\
\hline
6 \leq \text{maxOnCourse} \wedge \text{maxOnCourse} \leq 30 \\
\end{array}$$

or

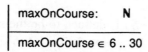

Schemas can make reference to *capacity* and *maxOnCourse* without explicitly including their defining schemas:

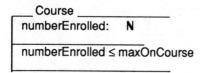

If a schema contains several lines of declarations then each line is regarded as being terminated by a semicolon. Furthermore, if the predicate part consists of more than one line then the lines are regarded as being joined by *and* operators. For example

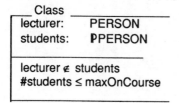

is the same as

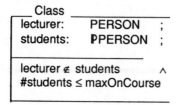

Schema calculus

Schemas can be regarded as units and manipulated by various operators which are analogous to those of predicate calculus.

Decoration

The schema S decorated with a prime S', is defined to be the same as S with all its observations decorated with a prime. It is used to signify the value of a schema after some operation has been carried out.

```
┌─ S' ─────────────────────
│ a', b':        N
│─────────────────────────
│ a' < b'
└─────────────────────────
```

Inclusion

The name of a schema can be included in the declarations of another schema. The effect is for the included schema to be *textually imported*; its declarations are merged with those of the including schema and its predicate part is conjoined ('*and*ed') with that of the including schema.

```
┌─ IncludeS ───────────────
│ c:             N
│ S
│─────────────────────────
│ c < 10
└─────────────────────────
```

means

```
┌─ IncludeS ───────────────
│ c:             N
│ a, b:          N
│─────────────────────────
│ c < 10
│ a < b
└─────────────────────────
```

Schema conjunction

Two schemas can be joined by an *and* operator. The effect is to make a new schema with the declarations of the two component schemas merged and their predicates conjoined ('*and*ed'). Given S as before and T:

```
┌─ T ──────────────────────
│ b, c:          N
│─────────────────────────
│ b < c
└─────────────────────────
```

SandT ≙ S ∧ T

means

```
 ___ SandT _____
|  a, b, c:        N
|_____
|  a < b
|  b < c
|_____
```

Observations with the same name, such as the two *b*'s here, are merged if they have the same type. If not then the schema conjunction is illegal.

Schema disjunction

Two schemas can be joined by an *or* operator. The effect is to make a new schema with the declarations of the two component schemas merged and their predicates disjoined ('*or*ed'). Given *S* and *T* as before:

SorT ≙ S ∨ T

means

```
 ___ SorT _____
|  a, b, c:        N
|_____
|  a < b ∨ b < c
|_____
```

Implication

A similar joining is possible using implication. Given *S* and *T* as before

SimplT ≙ S ⇒ T

means

```
 ___ SimplT _____
|  a, b, c:        N
|_____
|  a < b ⇒ b < c
|_____
```

Equivalence

Finally, a similar joining is possible using equivalence. Given S and T as before:

$$\text{SeqT} \triangleq S \Leftrightarrow T$$

means

```
┌─ SeqT ──────────────
│ a, b, c:      N
├─────────────────────
│ a < b ⇔ b < c
│
└─────────────────────
```

Delta convention

The convention that the value of an observation before an operation is denoted by the undecorated name of the observation, and the value after an operation by the name decorated by a prime (') character, is used in the *delta* naming convention. By convention a schema with the Greek character capital delta (Δ) as the first character of its name, such as ΔS, is defined to be:

$$\Delta S \triangleq S \wedge S'$$

```
┌─ ΔS ────────────────
│ a, b          N
│ a', b':       N
├─────────────────────
│ a < b
│ a' < b'
└─────────────────────
```

The delta in ΔS is used, as in other areas of mathematics, to signify a change in S. Unless a document uses a schema name with a Δ as the first character with some other significance, there is no need to define the significance of the Δ explicitly. In other words, having defined a schema S, one can use ΔS without defining it, so long as the conventional meaning is to be assigned to it.

Xi convention

By convention a schema with the Greek character capital *xi* (Ξ) as the first character of its name, such as Ξ*S*, is defined to be:

```
__ ΞS _____
 a, b        N
 a', b':     N
 _____
 a < b
 a' < b'
 a = a'
 b = b'
|_____
```

The xi in Ξ*S* is used because of its similarity in appearance to the equivalence symbol ≡ and it signifies the state of *S* before and after an operation where no change takes place to any of *S*'s observations. Unless a document uses a schema name with a Ξ as the first character with some other significance, there is no need to define the significance of the Ξ explicitly.

Decoration of input and output observations

A convention is used to decorate the observations of a schema which specifies an operation. Finishing the observation's name with a question mark (?) indicates that the observation is an *input* to the schema. Finishing the observation's name with an exclamation mark (!) indicates that the observation is an *output* from the schema. Note that the question mark and exclamation mark are simply characters in the observation's name.

Simple example of schema with input and output

```
__ Add _____
 a?, b?:     N
 sum!:       N
 _____
 sum! = a? + b?
|_____
```

Example of schemas with input

The display of a computer terminal shows lines of characters with each line consisting of a fixed number of columns containing a character in a fixed-width typeface. A *cursor* marks a current position of interest on the display. The user can type *keys*, some of which directly control the position of the cursor.

[KEY]   the set of keys on the terminal's keyboard

> numLines: **N**
> numColumns: **N**
> ---
> 1 ≤ numLines
> 1 ≤ numColumns

The lines are numbered from 1 to *numLines* down the display and the columns are numbered 1 to *numColumns* across the display.

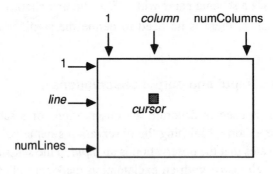

Figure 6.1

The state

At any time the cursor is within the bounds of the display. The state of the cursor can be described by the schema *Cursor*

> ___ Cursor _____
> line: **N**
> column: **N**
> ---
> line ∈ 1 .. numLines
> column ∈ 1 .. numColumns

Special keys

The operations for moving a cursor involve distinguishing the key pressed. For this we define six special values of type *KEY*. There is no need to give their actual values but these must all be different.

> left, right, up, down,
> home, return: KEY
> ───────────────────────
> disjoint ⟨ {left}, {right}, {up}, {down}, {home}, {return} ⟩

Home key

The operations for moving the cursor can be built up one at a time. The most simple is the reponse to the *home* key. It causes the cursor to move to the top left corner of the display.

> ┌─── HomeKey ─────────────
> │ ΔCursor
> │ key?:   KEY
> ├─────────────────────────
> │ key? = home
> │ line' = 1
> │ column' = 1
> └─────────────────────────

The schema *ΔCursor* is defined by convention to be:

> ┌─── ΔCursor ─────────────
> │ line, line':   N
> │ column, column':   N
> ├─────────────────────────
> │ line ∈ 1 .. numLines
> │ line' ∈ 1 .. numLines
> │ column ∈ 1 .. numColumns
> │ column' ∈ 1 .. numColumns
> └─────────────────────────

Down key

The action for responding to the *down* key is given next. It causes the cursor to move to the same column position on the next line down. It is easiest to start by dealing with what happens if the cursor is not on the bottom line of the display.

```
┌─── DownKeyNormal ──────
│ ΔCursor
│ key?:          KEY
├────────────────────────
│ key? = down
│ line < numLines
│ line' = line + 1
│ column' = column
│
└────────────────────────
```

The next schema deals with what happens when the cursor is on the bottom line of the display.

```
┌─── DownKeyAtBottom ────
│ ΔCursor
│ key?:          KEY
├────────────────────────
│ key? = down
│ line = numLines
│ line' = 1
│ column' = column
│
└────────────────────────
```

Note that the cursor has been defined to *wrap round* to the top line of the display.

The full behaviour is given by

$$DownKey \triangleq DownKeyNormal \lor DownKeyAtBottom$$

Up key

The response to the *up* key can be defined in a similar manner and is left as an exercise for the reader.

Return key

The response to the *return* key is to move to the leftmost column of the next line down or the top line if the cursor was on the bottom line. For contrast this is given as a single schema

```
┌─── ReturnKey ──────────────
│ ΔCursor
│ key?:        KEY
├────────────────────────
│ key? = return
│ column' = 1
│ ((line < numLines ∧ line' = line + 1)
│ ∨
│   (line = numLines ∧ line' = 1))
└────────────────────────
```

Right key

Next the operation for moving right is given. It is easiest to deal first with what happens when the cursor is not at the far right of the display:

```
┌─── RightKeyNormal ────────
│ ΔCursor
│ key?:        KEY
├────────────────────────
│ key? = right
│ column < numColumns
│ column' = column + 1
│ line' = line
└────────────────────────
```

The next schema deals with the cursor's being at the end of a line other than the bottom line of the display. Note that the cursor wraps round to the start of the next line

```
┌─── RightKeyAtEnd ─────────
│ ΔCursor
│ key?:        KEY
├────────────────────────
│ key? = right
│ column = numColumns
│ column' = 1
│ line < numLines
│ line' = line + 1
└────────────────────────
```

Finally a separate schema deals with the cursor's being at the end of the bottom line. The cursor wraps round to the left of the top line:

```
┌── RightKeyAtBottom ──────
│ ΔCursor
│ key?:        KEY
├──────────────────
│ key? = right
│ column = numColumns
│ column' = 1
│ line = numLines
│ line' = 1
│
└
```

These schemas can be combined to form one schema which defines the response of the cursor to a right-move key in all initial positions of the cursor

$$RightKey \triangleq RightKeyNormal \lor RightKeyAtEnd \lor RightKeyAtBottom$$

For the sake of illustration here is the expansion of *RightKey*

```
┌── RightKey──────────────
│ ΔCursor
│ key?:        KEY
├──────────────────
│ (key? = right
│ column < numColumns
│ column' = column + 1
│ line' = line)
│
│ ∨
│ (key? = right
│ column = numColumns
│ column' = 1
│ line < numLines
│ line' = line + 1)
│
│ ∨
│ (key? = right
│ column = numColumns
│ column' = 1
│ line = numLines
│ line' = 1)
│
└
```

This can be simplified to

```
┌─── RightKey ─────────────────
│ ΔCursor
│ key?:          KEY
├─────────────────────────────
│ key? = right
│ ∧
│ ((column < numColumns
│   column' = column + 1
│   line' = line)
│
│  ∨
│  (column = numColumns
│   column' = 1
│    (line < numLines
│     line' = line + 1)
│
│  ∨
│   (line = numLines
│     line' = 1)
│  ))
│
└─────────────────────────────
```

Of course the behaviour of the cursor at the end of the line and at bottom right of the display need not be defined as here. The style used here of defining separate schemas to describe the behaviour in these situations makes it easier to understand what happens in these cases.

Left key

The action of the cursor for moving left can be defined in a similar way by a schema *LeftKey*. This is left as an exercise.

Cursor-control keys

The action of the cursor on the pressing of any of these *cursor-control* keys can be defined by

$$CursorControlKey \,\hat{=}\,$$
$$HomeKey \lor ReturnKey \lor UpKey \lor DownKey \lor LeftKey \lor RightKey$$

Overall structure of a Z specification document

A Z specification document consists of mathematical text in the Z notation, interleaved with explanatory text in a natural language. The explanatory text should be expressed in terms of the problem and should not refer directly to the mathematical formulation. This rule is broken only in the case of documents intended as tutorials on Z.

Sections of a Z document

The sections of a Z document are as follows:

• Introduction

• The types used in the specification

• The state and its invariant properties

• An initial state

• Operations and enquiries

• Error handling

• Final versions of operations and enquiries

 A simple example of a Z specification document appears in the next chapter.

Summary of notation

```
___ SchemaName _____
declarations
_____
predicate
```

SchemaName ≜ [declarations | predicate]

Axiomatic definition

```
declarations
_____
predicate
```

Inclusion

```
┌─ IncludeS ──────────────
│ c:           N
│ S
├─────────────────────────
│ c < 10
│
└─────────────────────────
```

≙

```
┌─ IncludeS ──────────────
│ c:           N
│ a, b:        N
├─────────────────────────
│ c < 10
│ a < b
└─────────────────────────
```

Conjunction

```
┌─ T ─────────────────────
│ b, c:        N
├─────────────────────────
│ b < c
│
└─────────────────────────
```

SandT ≙ S ∧ T

≙

```
┌─ SandT ─────────────────
│ a, b, c:     N
├─────────────────────────
│ a < b
│ b < c
└─────────────────────────
```

Disjunction

SorT ≙ S ∨ T

≙

```
┌─ SorT ──────────────────
│ a, b, c:     N
├─────────────────────────
│ a < b ∨ b < c
│
└─────────────────────────
```

Implication

SimpIT ≙ S ⇒ T

≙

```
___ SimpIT _____
| a, b, c:        N
|_____
| a < b ⇒ b < c
|_____
```

Equivalence

SeqT ≙ S ⇔ T

≙

```
___ SeqT _____
| a, b, c:        N
|_____
| a < b ⇔ b < c
|_____
```

Decoration

```
___ S _____
| a, b:           N
|_____
| a < b
|_____
```

```
___ S' _____
| a', b':         N
|_____
| a' < b'
|_____
```

Exercises

6.1) Define a schema *LinesRemaining* which delivers the number of lines below the cursor as an output parameter.

Make use of schemas from the examples in this chapter.

6.2) Define a schema *UpKey* to define the operation of pressing the *up* key.

6.3) Define a schema *LeftKey* to define the operation of pressing the *left* key.

6.4) Devise a schema to define pressing the *down* key where the cursor does not move at all if it is already on the bottom line of the screen.

Make use of schemas from the examples in this chapter and from your solutions to the previous exercises.

6.5) Devise a schema to define pressing the *right* key where the cursor does not move at all if it is already on the last column of the screen.

Make use of schemas from the examples in this chapter and from your solutions to the previous exercises.

7   An example of a Z specification document

Introduction

This specification concerns recording the passengers aboard an aircraft. There are no seat numbers; passengers are allowed aboard on a first-come-first-served basis.

The types

The only *basic type* involved here is the set of all possible persons, *PERSON*:

[PERSON]   the set of all possible uniquely identified persons

The aircraft has a fixed capacity:

capacity: $\mathbb{N}$

The state

The state of the system is given by the set of persons on board the aircraft. The number of persons on board must never exceed the capacity. This is the state's *invariant* property.

```
__ Aircraft _____
onboard:    ℙPERSON
_____
#onboard ≤ capacity
_____
```

The state before and after an operation is described by the schema $\Delta Aircraft$, which has its conventional meaning:

```
┌─ ΔAircraft ──────────────
│ onboard:     ℙPERSON
│ onboard':    ℙPERSON
├──────────────────────────
│ #onboard ≤ capacity
│ #onboard' ≤ capacity
└──────────────────────────
```

Initial state

There must be an initial state for the system. The obvious one is where the aircraft is empty:

```
┌─ Init ────────────────────
│ Aircraft
├───────────────────────────
│ onboard = ∅
└───────────────────────────
```

The initial state must satisfy the state's invariant property. This it clearly does, since the size of the empty set is zero, which is less than or equal to all natural numbers and so to all possible values of *capacity*.

Operations

Boarding

There must be an operation to allow a person $p?$ to board the aircraft. A first version of this is called $Board_0$:

```
┌─ Board₀ ──────────────────
│ ΔAircraft
│ p?:          PERSON
├───────────────────────────
│ p? ∉ onboard
│ #onboard < capacity
│ onboard' = onboard ∪ {p?}
└───────────────────────────
```

Disembarking

It is also necessary to have an operation to allow a person $p?$ to disembark from the aircraft. A first version of this is $Disembark_0$:

```
__ Disembark₀ _____
ΔAircraft
p?:              PERSON
_____
p? ∈ onboard
onboard' = onboard \ {p?}
```

Enquiry operations

These operations leave the state unchanged and therefore use the schema:

ΞAircraft

which has its conventional meaning:

```
__ ΞAircraft _____
onboard:     ℙPERSON
onboard':    ℙPERSON
_____
#onboard ≤ capacity
#onboard' ≤ capacity
onboard = onboard'
```

Number on board

In addition to operations which change the state of the system it is necessary to have an operation to discover the number of persons on board:

```
__ Number _____
ΞAircraft
numOnBoard!:     N
_____
numOnBoard! = #onboard
```

Person on board

Furthermore, a useful enquiry is to discover whether or not a given person *p* ? is on board. The data type *YESORNO* is defined to provide suitable values for the reply and is used in the schema *OnBoard*:

YESORNO ::= yes | no

```
__ OnBoard_____
| ΞAircraft
| p?:          PERSON
| reply!:      YESORNO
|_____
| (p? ∈ onboard ∧ reply! = yes)
| ∨
| (p? ∉ onboard ∧ reply! = no)
|
```

Dealing with errors

The schemas $Board_0$ and $Disembark_0$ do not state what happens if their preconditions are not satisfied. The schema calculus of Z allows these schemas to be extended, firstly to give a message in the event of success:

RESPONSE ::=
  OK | alreadyOnBoard | full | notOnBoard | twoErrors

OKMESSAGE ≙ [rep!: RESPONSE| rep! = OK]

Boarding

A schema to handle errors *BoardError* is defined. It causes no change to the value of *onboard*, so the schema *ΞAircraft* is used:

```
__ BoardError_____
| ΞAircraft
| p?:          PERSON
| rep!:        RESPONSE
|_____
| (p? ∈ onboard ∧
| #onboard = capacity ∧
| rep! = twoErrors)
| ∨ (p? ∈ onboard ∧
| #onboard < capacity ∧
| rep! = alreadyOnBoard)
| ∨ (p? ∉ onboard ∧
| #onboard = capacity ∧
| rep! = full)
|
```

Finally *Board* can be defined:

$$Board \triangleq (Board_0 \wedge OKMESSAGE) \vee BoardError$$

Disembark

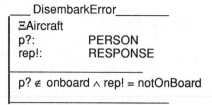

```
___ DisembarkError_____
  ΞAircraft
  p?:           PERSON
  rep!:         RESPONSE
 _____
  p? ∉ onboard ∧ rep! = notOnBoard
```

Finally *Disembark* can be defined:

$$Disembark \triangleq (Disembark_0 \wedge OKMessage) \vee DisembarkError$$

Exercises

Using the style of this chapter, create the following components of a formal specification for the computer example of exercise 2.1 and later:

7.1) The types and the schema for the state.

7.2) The operation to add a user.

7.3) The operation to remove a user.

7.4) The operation to log in.

7.5) The operation to log out.

8 Logic: predicate calculus

Introduction

A *predicate* is a statement which depends on a value or values. When a predicate is applied to a particular value it becomes a proposition. An example is the predicate

   prime(x)

which depends on some numeric value x, so that

   prime(7)

is a true proposition meaning that seven is a prime number, and

   prime(6)

is a false proposition.

Quantifiers

Quantifiers can be applied to predicates to give propositions.

Universal quantifier

The *universal quantifier* is written:

   $\forall$

and is pronounced "for all" (it looks like an upside-down 'A', in *for All*). It is used in the form:

∀ declaration | constraint • predicate

which states that for the declaration(s) given, restricted to certain values (by a predicate called a constraint), the predicate holds.

For each of the quantifiers to be described here, the

| constraint

part may be omitted.

The declaration introduces a typical variable which is then optionally constrained. The predicate applies to this variable. For example, to state that all natural numbers less than 10 have squares less than 100:

∀ i: N | i < 10 • i² < 100

This would be pronounced: "for all *i* drawn from the set of natural numbers, such that *i* is under ten, *i* squared is less than 100".

Existential quantifier

The *existential quantifier* is written:

∃

and is pronounced "there exists" (it looks like a backwards 'E', in *there Exists*). It is used in the form:

∃ declaration | constraint • predicate

The declaration introduces a typical variable which is then optionally constrained. The predicate applies to this variable. For example, to state that there is a natural number under ten which has a square less than 100:

∃ i: N | i < 10 • i² < 100

This would be pronounced: "there exists an *i* drawn from the set of natural numbers, such that *i* is less than ten, and *i* squared is less than 100".

Note that there need not be only one value of *i* for which this is true; in this example there are ten: 0 to 9.

To define the predicate *Even*:

Even(x) == ∃ k: **Z** • k * 2 = x

Unique quantifier

The *unique quantifier* is similar to the existential quantifier except that it states that there exists *only one* value for which the predicate is true.

The unique quantifier is written:

∃₁

An example is:

∃₁ i: **N** | i < 10 • i² < 100 ∧ i² > 80

This would be pronounced: "there exists only one *i* drawn from the set of natural numbers, where *i* is less than ten, such that *i* squared is less than 100 and *i* squared is greater than 80". It is equivalent to saying that the predicate holds for *i*, but that there is no *j* (with a value different from *i*) for which it holds:

∃₁ i: **N** | i < 10 • i² < 100 ∧ i² > 80

==

∃ i: **N** | i < 10 • i² < 100 ∧ i² > 80
∧ ¬(∃ j: **N** | j < 10 ∧ i ≠ j • j² < 100 ∧ j² > 80)

Counting quantifier

Some notations use a counting quantifier which counts for how many values of the variable the predicate holds. In Z this is not needed; instead one uses a set comprehension to construct the set of values for which the predicate holds, and then finds the size of the set.

An example is: the number of natural numbers under ten which have squares greater than thirty:

$$\# \{ i: \mathbb{N} \mid i < 10 \bullet i^2 > 30 \}$$

Further operations on schemas

Renaming

The observations in a schema may be *renamed* by the following form:

schemaName [newName / oldName]

For example, given:

```
__Aircraft_____
onboard:    ℙPERSON
_____
#onboard ≤ capacity
```

then

Ship ≙ Aircraft [passengers / onboard]

gives:

```
__Ship_____
passengers: ℙPERSON
_____
#passengers ≤ capacity
```

Quantifiers in schema

Quantifiers may be used in the expressions contained in the predicate part of a schema.

Hiding

The schema *hiding* operator hides specified variables so that they are no longer variables of the schema and simply become local variables of existential operators in the predicate part of the schema. For example, given:

```
  ┌─ S ─────────────────
  │ a:          N
  │ b:          N
  │ ─────────────────
  │ a < b
  └─────────────────────
```

then

BHidden ≙ S \ (b)

gives the schema:

```
  ┌─ BHidden ───────────
  │ a:          N
  │ ─────────────────
  │ ∃ b: N • a < b
  └─────────────────────
```

Several variable names can be given in the brackets.

Projection

Schema *projection* is similar to hiding except *all but* the named variables are hidden. Given S as above then

AProjected ≙ S ↾ (a)

gives the schema:

```
  ┌─ AProjected ────────
  │ a:          N
  │ ─────────────────
  │ ∃ b: N • a < b
  └─────────────────────
```

Pre

The *precondition* of a schema

pre schemaName

is constructed by hiding all variables of the schema that correspond to *after* states (decorated with ') and all those which are outputs (decorated with !). Given the full definition of the operation to disembark from the aircraft:

```
┌── Disembark ──────────────
│ onboard:     ℙPERSON
│ onboard':    ℙPERSON
│ p?:          PERSON
│ rep!:        RESPONSE
├───────────────────────────
│ #onboard ≤ capacity
│ #onboard' ≤ capacity
│
│ (p? ∈ onboard ∧ rep! = OK
│   onboard' = onboard ∪ { p? })
│ ∨
│ (p? ∉ onboard ∧ rep! = notOnBoard
│   onboard' = onboard)
└───────────────────────────
```

then the precondition

pre Disembark

would be:

Disembark \ (onboard', rep!)

which is

```
┌── pre Disembark ──────────
│ onboard:     ℙPERSON
│ p?:          PERSON
├───────────────────────────
│ #onboard ≤ capacity
│ ∃ rep!: RESPONSE; onboard': ℙPERSON •
│ (#onboard' ≤ capacity
│   (p? ∈ onboard ∧ rep! = OK
│   onboard' = onboard ∪ { p? })
│ ∨
│ (p? ∉ onboard ∧ rep! = notOnBoard
│   onboard' = onboard))
└───────────────────────────
```

Schema composition

The *composition* of schema S with schema T is written:

$$S \, \mathbin{;} T$$

and signifies the effect of doing S, then doing T. It is equivalent to renaming the variables describing the after state of S to some temporary names and the equivalent variables describing the before state of T with the same temporary names and then hiding the temporary names.

For example to show the effect of pressing the right key and then the left key on a visual display, using the definition of *CursorControlKey* from Chapter 6:

PressRight $\triangleq$ CursorControlKey $\wedge$ [key?: KEY | key? = right]
PressLeft $\triangleq$ CursorControlKey $\wedge$ [key?: KEY | key? = left]

PressRight $\mathbin{;}$ PressLeft
$\triangleq$

PressRight [tempCol / column', tempLine / line'] $\wedge$
PressLeft [tempCol / column, tempLine / line]
\ (tempCol, tempLine)

Summary of notation

$\forall \, x: T \bullet P_x$ Universal quantification:
"for all x of type T, P_x holds"

$\exists \, x: T \bullet P_x$ Existential quantification:
"there exists an x of type T, such that P_x holds"

$\exists_1 \, x: T \bullet P_x$ Unique existence:
"there exists a unique x of type T, such that P_x holds"
$== (\exists \, x: T \bullet P_x \wedge \neg(\exists \, y: T \mid x \neq y \bullet P_y \,))$

S[new / old,...]	schema renaming
S \ (x$_1$, x$_2$,...,x$_n$)	schema hiding
S ↾ (x$_1$, x$_2$,...,x$_n$)	schema projection
pre S	precondition of S
S ⨾ T	schema composition: S, then T

Exercises

8.1) Express the statement

loggedIn ⊆ users

by using universal quantification over all persons.

8.2) Use quantification to express the fact that if the set *users* is not empty, then there is at least one user.

8.3) Use quantification to express the fact that if the size of the set *users* is one, then there is precisely one user.

8.4) Given the predicate divisible, defined

divisible(m, n) == m mod n = 0

define a predicate

prime(n)

which is true if *n* is a prime number. (That is, has no divisors except itself and one).

8.5) Use schemas which are already available from this text and from your previous answers, to construct a schema *Government* which represents the fact that a parliament consists of a set of politicians, and that some members of the parliament are in the Cabinet.

9 Relations

A relation is a set

The examples considered so far have been limited to one basic type which means that the specifications cannot develop to be any more sophisticated. What is needed is some way of relating sets to one another. This can be done by means of a *relation*, which is based on the idea of a *Cartesian product*.

Cartesian Product

A *Cartesian product* , named after the French mathematician Descartes, is a combination of two or more sets. The Cartesian product of the sets X, Y and Z would be written:

$$X \times Y \times Z$$

and pronounced "the Cartesian product of X, Y and Z" or "X cross Y cross Z". Values drawn from this combination of types are called *tuples* and are written:

$$(x, y, z)$$

where x is of type X, y of type Y and z of type Z.

Such a tuple is called *ordered* since the order of writing the components is important.

A tuple formed from two types is called a *pair* and a tuple formed from three types is called a *triple*. A tuple of n types is sometimes called an *n-tuple*.

An example of a tuple (a 4-tuple) connects information about a person:

NAME × ADDRESS × **N** × TELEPHONE

to record name, address, age and telephone-number.

Relations

A special case of a Cartesian product is a *pair*. A *binary* relation is a set of pairs, of related values.

For example, a relation called *speaks* between countries and languages spoken in those countries can be thought of as a set of pairs. Given:

[COUNTRY]   the set of all countries
[LANGUAGE]   the set of all languages

part of the value of this set might be

{(France, French), (Canada, French),
(Canada, English), (Great Britain, English), (USA, English)}

A relation can be illustrated by a diagram called a *directed graph* or *digraph*.

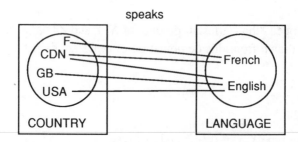

Figure 9.1

Such a set could be declared:

speaks: **P**(COUNTRY × LANGUAGE)

Note that there are no restrictions requiring values of the two sets to be paired only one to one; relations pair *many* to *many*. For example it would be quite acceptable to have the relation:

{(France, French), (Germany, German), (Austria, German),
(Switzerland, French), (Switzerland, German),
(Switzerland, Italian), (Switzerland, Romansch)}

Furthermore there is no particular reason to choose to relate the values in this direction; one could as well relate language to country, by declaring:

spoken: $\mathbb{P}$(LANGUAGE $\times$ COUNTRY)

Declaring a relation

The idea of a relation is reinforced by the use of the two-headed arrow in the alternative, conventional style of declaration:

R: X $\leftrightarrow$ Y
speaks: COUNTRY $\leftrightarrow$ LANGUAGE

These can be pronounced: "*R* relates *X* to *Y*" and "*speaks* relates country to language".

Note the following equivalences:

X $\leftrightarrow$ Y == $\mathbb{P}$(X $\times$ Y)

speaks: COUNTRY $\leftrightarrow$ LANGUAGE
==
speaks: $\mathbb{P}$(COUNTRY $\times$ LANGUAGE)

Maplets

The idea of a related pair is reinforced by the conventional notation for one pair in a relation, a *maplet*:

x $\mapsto$ y == (x, y)

pronounced "x is related to y" or "x maps to y"

United Kingdom ↦ English ∈ speaks
== (United Kingdom, English) ∈ speaks

The set of pairs given above could alternatively be written as a set of maplets:

{France ↦ French, Germany ↦ German, Austria ↦ German,
Switzerland ↦ French, Switzerland ↦ German,
Switzerland ↦ Italian, Switzerland ↦ Romansch}

Membership

To discover if a certain pair of values are related it is sufficient to see if the pair or maplet is an element of the relation:

(United Kingdom, English) ∈ speaks

or

United Kingdom ↦ English ∈ speaks

Equivalently, the name of the relation can be used as an *infix* operator:

United Kingdom speaks English

In general:

x R y == x ↦ y ∈ R == (x, y) ∈ R

Domain and range

A relation relates values of a set called the *source* or *from-set* to values of a set called the *target* or *to-set*. In the example:

R: X ↔ Y

the source is X and the target is Y and in the example:

speaks: COUNTRY ↔ LANGUAGE

the source is *COUNTRY* and the target is *LANGUAGE*.

In most cases only a subset of the source is involved in the relation. This subset is called the *domain* and is written *dom*. Usually only a subset of the target is involved in a relation. This subset is called the *range* and written *ran* (or sometimes *rng*).

In the example

> R: X ↔ Y

the domain of R

> dom R

is the subset containing those values of *X* which are related by *R* to values of *Y*. The range of *R*

> ran R

is the subset containing those values of *Y* which are related by *R* to values of *X*.

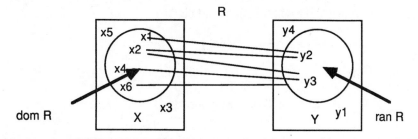

Figure 9.2

The domain of the relation *speaks*

> dom speaks

is the set of those countries where at least one language is spoken, and the range of *speaks*

> ran speaks

is that set of languages which are spoken in at least one country.

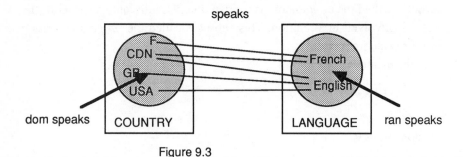

Figure 9.3

Relational image

To discover the set of values from the range of a relation related to a set of values from the domain of the relation one can use the *relational image*:

R (S)

pronounced "the relational image of *S* in *R*". For example, the languages spoken in France and Switzerland would be:

speaks ({France, Switzerland})

which is the set

{French, German, Italian, Romansch}

Constant value for a relation

Some relations have constant values. If the value of the relation is known, it can be given by an *axiomatic definition*. For example to define the relation greater-than-or-equal-to (≥):

$$\geq\ : N \leftrightarrow N$$

$$\forall i, j: N \bullet i \geq j \Leftrightarrow \exists n: N \bullet i = j + n$$

Where convenient several relations can be combined in one definition:

$$
\begin{array}{|l}
\_\geq\_ : N \leftrightarrow N \\
\_>\_ : N \leftrightarrow N \\
\hline
\forall i, j: N \bullet \\
i \geq j \Leftrightarrow \exists\, n: N \bullet i = j + n \\
i > j \Leftrightarrow \exists\, n: N_1 \bullet i = j + n
\end{array}
$$

The low-line (_) characters are used here to indicate that the relations ($\geq$) and ($>$) apply to two values.

Example of a relation

Public holidays around the world can be described as follows:

[COUNTRY]	the set of all the countries of the world
[DATE]	the dates of a given year

The relationship between countries and the dates of the country's public holidays is the relation *holidays*:

$$
\begin{array}{|l}
\_\_\_ \text{ Hols } _____ \\
\text{holidays:} \quad \text{COUNTRY} \leftrightarrow \text{DATE} \\
\hline
\end{array}
$$

An operation to discover whether a date *d?* is a public holiday in country *c?* is:

REPLY ::= yes | no

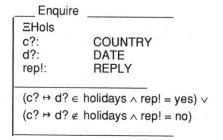

$$
\begin{array}{|l}
\_\_\_ \text{ Enquire } _____ \\
\Xi\text{Hols} \\
\text{c?:} \qquad \text{COUNTRY} \\
\text{d?:} \qquad \text{DATE} \\
\text{rep!:} \qquad \text{REPLY} \\
\hline
(\text{c?} \mapsto \text{d?} \in \text{holidays} \wedge \text{rep!} = \text{yes}) \vee \\
(\text{c?} \mapsto \text{d?} \notin \text{holidays} \wedge \text{rep!} = \text{no})
\end{array}
$$

An operation to decree a public holiday in country *c?* on date *d?* is:

```
___ Decree _____
| ΔHols
| c?:          COUNTRY
| d?:          DATE
|_____
| holidays' = holidays ∪ {c? ↦ d?}
|_____
```

Note that *Decree* ignores the possibility of the date's already being a public holiday in that country.

An operation to abolish a public holiday in country *c?* on date *d?* is:

```
___ Abolish _____
| ΔHols
| c?:          COUNTRY
| d?:          DATE
|_____
| holidays' = holidays \ {c? ↦ d?}
|_____
```

Note that *Abolish* ignores the possibility of the date's not already being a public holiday in that country.

An operation to find the dates *ds!* of all the public holidays in country *c?* is:

```
___ Dates _____
| ΞHols
| c?:          COUNTRY
| ds!:         ℙDATE
|_____
| ds! = holidays (| {c?} |)
|_____
```

Restriction

Further operators are available, to *restrict* a relation.

Domain restriction

The *domain restriction* operator restricts a relation to that part where the domain is contained in a particular set:

$$S ◁ R$$

"the relation R domain restricted to S".

In terms of the digraph the "point" of the operator can be thought of as pointing left to the domain.

Range restriction

The *range restriction* operator restricts a relation to that part where the range is contained in a set:

$$R \triangleright S$$

"the relation R range restricted to S".

The point of the operator can be thought of as pointing right to the range.

Domain anti-restriction

The domain anti-restriction operator restricts a relation to that part where the domain is *not* contained in a set:

$$S \triangleleft R$$

"the relation R domain anti-restricted to S".

The point of the operator can be thought of as pointing left to the domain.

Domain anti-restriction is also known as domain *co-restriction*, or domain *subtraction*.

Range anti-restriction

The range anti-restriction operator restricts a relation to that part where the range is *not* contained in a set:

$$R \triangleright S$$

"the relation R range anti-restricted to S".

The point of the operator can be thought of as pointing right to the range.

Range anti-restriction is also known as range *co-restriction*, or range *subtraction*.

Example of restriction

Given the set of all countries and the set of dates and the relation *holidays* as before and the set of countries in the European Community *EC*

EC: ℙCOUNTRY

the relation mapping only EC countries to their public holidays is:

EC ◁ holidays

and the relation mapping *non*-EC countries to their public holidays is:

EC ◁ holidays

Given a subset of dates *summer*

summer: ℙDATE

the relation of countries to public holidays in the summer is

holidays ▷ summer

and the relation of countries to public holidays *not* in the summer is

holidays ▷ summer

Composition

Relations can be joined together by an operation called *composition*. Given a relation *R* which relates *X* to *Y*

R: X ↔ Y

and a relation *Q* which relates *Y* to *Z*

Q: Y ↔ Z

the following compositions are possible:

Forward composition

The relation formed by the relation R, then the relation Q, is called the *forward composition* of R with Q:

R: X ↔ Y
Q: Y ↔ Z

R ; Q: X ↔ Z

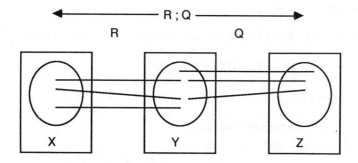

Figure 9.4

For any pair *(x, z)* related by R forward composed with Q

x R ; Q z

there is a y where R relates x to y and Q relates y to z:

∃ y: Y • x R y ∧ y Q z

Backward composition

The *backward composition* of Q with R. It is the same as the forward composition of R with Q:

Q ∘ R == R ; Q

It is similar to the mathematical notion of *functional composition*.

Repeated composition

A *homogeneous* relation is one which relates values from a type to values of *the same type* (the source and the target are the same). Such a relation can be composed with itself:

R: X ↔ X

R ; R: X ↔ X

Example

Countries are related by the relation *borders* if they share a border

borders: COUNTRY ↔ COUNTRY

For example:

France borders Switzerland
Switzerland borders Austria

Countries are related by *borders* composed with *borders*

borders ; borders

if they each share a border with a third country

France borders ; borders Austria

since France borders Germany and Germany borders Austria.
This can also be written:

France borders^2 Austria

Furthermore:

Spain borders^3 Denmark

means

Spain borders ; borders ; borders Denmark

In general

    x R⁺ y

means that there is a repeated composition of R which relates x to y.
  For example:

    France borders⁺ India   which is true

means that France is on the same landmass as India.

Identity relation

The *identity relation*

    id X

is the relation which maps all x's on to themselves:

    id X == {x: X • x ↦ x}

  The repeated composition

    R˙

includes the identity relation.

Inverse of a relation

The inverse of a relation R from X to Y

    R: X ↔ Y

is written

    R˜   (sometimes R⁻¹)

and is the same relation "in the other direction", that is from X to Y, so if

    x R y

then

$$y \; R^\sim \; x$$

Examples

Family relationships can be defined by means of the notation introduced in this chapter:

Definitions

[PERSON]   the set of all persons

father, mother: PERSON $\leftrightarrow$ PERSON

with suitable values and with interpretations:

x father y

and

v mother w

meaning "*x* has *y* as father" and "*v* has *w* as mother"

Parent

The relation *parent* (mother or father)

parent: PERSON $\leftrightarrow$ PERSON

can be defined as the union of the relations *father* and *mother*:

parent = father $\cup$ mother

Sibling

The relation *sibling* (brother or sister)

sibling: PERSON $\leftrightarrow$ PERSON

can be defined as the relation *parent* composed with its own inverse. In other words, the set of persons with the same parents. A person is not usually counted as their own sibling so the identity relation for *PERSON* is excluded:

sibling = (parent ; parent~) \ id PERSON

Ancestor

The relation *ancestor* can be defined as the repeated composition of *parent*:

ancestor: PERSON $\leftrightarrow$ PERSON

ancestor = parent+

Summary of notation

X, Y and Z are sets and x: X; y: Y; R: X $\leftrightarrow$ Y:

X $\times$ Y	the set of ordered pairs of X's and Y's
X $\leftrightarrow$ Y	the set of relations from X to Y: == $\mathbb{P}(X \times Y)$
x R y	x is related by R to y: == (x, y) $\in$ R
x $\mapsto$ y	== (x, y)
{ $x_1 \mapsto y_1, x_2 \mapsto y_2, \ldots, x_n \mapsto y_n$}	
	== the relation { (x_1, y_1), (x_2, y_2), ..., (x_n, y_n) }
	relating x_1 to y_1, x_2 to y_2, ..., x_n to y_n
dom R	the domain of a relation
	== {x: X | ($\exists$y: Y . x R y) • x}
ran R	the range of a relation
	== {y: Y | ($\exists$x: X . x R y) • y}
R (S)	the relational image of S in R
S $\lhd$ R	the relation R domain restricted to S
R $\rhd$ S	the relation R range restricted to S
S $\lhd\!\!\!-$ R	the relation R domain anti-restricted to S
R $-\!\!\!\rhd$ S	the relation R range anti-restricted to S
R ; Q	the forward composition of R with Q

Q ∘ R	the backward composition of Q with R
R+	the repeated self-composition of R
R*	the repeated self-composition of R with identity
	== R+ ∪ id X
R~	the inverse of R
id X	{x: X • x ↦ x}

Exercises

In all cases use definitions from this chapter.

9.1) Express the fact that the language Latin is not spoken in any country (as official language).

9.2) Express the fact that Switzerland has four official languages.

9.3) Give a value to the relation *speaksInEC* which relates countries which are in the set *EC* to their languages.

9.4) Give a value to the relation *grandparent*.

9.5) A person's first cousin (or full cousin or cousin-german) is defined as a child of the person's aunt or uncle.
  Give a value for the relation *firstCousin*.

10   Functions

A function is a relation

In a programming language a *function* is a way of specifying some processing which produces a value as a result. In Z a function is a data structure. These two views are not incompatible; the programming language view is just a restricted form of the Z view and in both cases a function provides a result value, given an input value or values.

A function is a special case of a relation in which there is *at most one* value in the range for each value in the domain. A function with a finite domain is also known as a *mapping*.

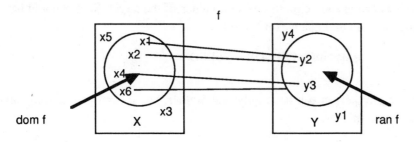

Figure 10.1

Note that in the diagram the lines *converge* from left to right.

In Z a function f from the type X to the type Y is declared by:

f: X ↛ Y

and is pronounced "the function f, from X to Y". This is equivalent to the relation f from X to Y:

f : X ↔ Y

with the restriction that for each x, f relates it to *at most one* y:

$$x \in \text{dom } f \Rightarrow \exists_1 y: Y \bullet x \, f \, y$$

Examples of functions

The relation between persons and identity numbers:

$$\text{identityNo}: \text{PERSON} \leftrightarrow \mathbb{N}$$

is a function if there is a rule that a person may only have one identity number. In this case it would be declared:

$$\text{identityNo}: \text{PERSON} \rightarrowtail \mathbb{N}$$

There would probably also be a rule that only one identity number may be associated with any person, but this is not indicated here.

Note that there is no restriction that the function must map different values of the source on to different values of the target. So one could have the function giving a person's mother:

$$\text{isMotherOf}: \text{PERSON} \rightarrowtail \text{PERSON}$$

since any person can have only one mother, but several people may have the same mother.

Function application

All the concepts which pertain to relations are also applicable to functions. In addition, however, a function may be *applied*. Since there will be at most one value in the range for a given x it is possible to designate that value directly. The value of f applied to x is the value in the range of the function f corresponding to the value x in its domain. The application is meaningless if the value of x is not in the domain of f.

The application of the function f to the value x (called its *argument*) is written:

$$f \, x$$

and pronounced "f of x" or "f applied to x".

Some people put brackets around the argument, as in:

f(x)

but although this is correct, it is not necessary.

Total and partial functions

The functions given as examples above have been shown as *partial*, which means that there are some values of the source which are not in the domain of the function. A *total* function is one where there is a value for every possible value of x, so $f\,x$ is always defined. The domain is the whole of the source.

A total function is declared by

f: X → Y

and is pronounced "f is a total function from X to Y". It is equivalent to

f : X ⇸ Y

"f is the partial function from X to Y", with the restriction that

dom f = X

Examples of total functions

The function *age,* from *PERSON* to natural numbers, is total since every person has an age:

age: PERSON → N

The function *isMotherOf* given above, is total since for any person there is exactly one person who is or was that person's mother:

isMotherOf: PERSON → PERSON

Other classes of functions

As well as their being either total or partial, other sorts of functions can be distinguished:

Injection

An *injection*, or *injective function*, is a function which maps different values of the source on to different values of the target. The inverse relation of an injective function *f*, from *X* to *Y*, *f˜*, is itself a function, from *Y* to *X*:

   f˜ ∈ Y ↣ X

An injective function may be partial or total. Injective functions are sometimes described as "one to one".

Since it is likely that each number is associated with only one person, the function *identityNo* given above would be injective.

Surjection

A *surjection*, or *surjective function*, is a function for which there is a value in the range for every value of the target; the range of the function is the target. Given the surjective function *f* from *X* to *Y*

   ran f = Y

A surjective function may be partial or total.

Bijection

A *bijection*, or *bijective function*, is one which maps every element of the source on to every element of the target in a one-to-one relationship. It is therefore: injective, total and surjective.

Arrow symbols

These classes of functions are distinguished by further arrow shapes. They are comparatively infrequently used and, since they are very similar to each other, can easily be confused. This book will not make use of any further arrow shapes but will state explicitly any special properties of any functions used.

Constant functions

Some functions are used as a means of providing a value, given a parameter or parameters. These are usually functions which maintain a *constant* mapping from their input parameters to their output values. If the value of the mapping is known, a value can be given to the function by an *axiomatic definition*. For example to define the function *square*:

$$\begin{array}{|l}
\text{square: } \mathbf{N} \rightarrow \mathbf{N} \\
\hline
\forall n\colon \mathbf{N} \cdot \text{square } n = n * n
\end{array}$$

Where convenient several functions can be combined in one definition:

$$\begin{array}{|l}
\text{square: } \mathbf{N} \rightarrow \mathbf{N} \\
\text{cube: } \mathbf{N} \rightarrow \mathbf{N} \\
\hline
\forall n\colon \mathbf{N} \cdot \\
\text{square } n = n * n \\
\text{cube } n = n * n * n
\end{array}$$

Functional overriding

A function can be modified by adding mapping pairs to it or by removing pairs. It can also be modified so that for a particular set of values of the domain it has new values in the range. This is called *overriding*. The function *f* overridden by the function *g* is written:

$$f \oplus g$$

It is the same as *f* for all values which are not in the domain of *g* and the same as *g* for all values which are in the domain of *g*:
If

$$x \in \text{dom } f \wedge x \notin \text{dom } g$$

then

$$f \oplus g\ x = f\ x$$

But if

$$x \in \text{dom } g$$

then

$$f \oplus g \, x = g \, x$$

An alternative definition is:

$$f \oplus g = (\text{dom } g \lhd f) \cup g$$

If *f* and *g* have disjoint domains

$$\text{dom } f \cap \text{dom } g = \emptyset$$

then

$$f \oplus g = f \cup g$$

Note: some users of Z allow overriding for relations.

Example of overriding

The recorded age of person *p?* is increased by 1:

$$\text{age} \oplus \{p? \mapsto \text{age } p? + 1\}$$

The function *age* is overridden by the function with only *p?* in its domain which maps to the former value plus one.

Example from business – stock control

A warehouse holds stocks of various items *carried* by an organisation. A computer system records the *level* of all items carried, the *withdrawal* of items from stock and the *delivery* of stock. Occasionally a new item will be carried and items will be discontinued, provided that their stock level is zero.

[ITEM]   the set of all items (item codes)

```
__ Warehouse _____
 carried:     ℙ ITEM
 level:        ITEM ⇸ ℕ
 _____
 dom level = carried
```

Every item carried has a level, even if it is zero.

```
__ Init _____
 Warehouse
 _____
 carried = Ø
 level = Ø
```

Initially there are no items.

```
__ WithDraw _____
 ΔWarehouse
 i?:          ITEM
 qty?:        ℕ
 _____
 i? ∈ carried
 level i? ≥ qty?
 level' = level ⊕ {i? ↦ level i? – qty?}
 carried' = carried
```

For a quantity of an item to be withdrawn, the item must be carried and there must be enough stock.

```
__ Deliver _____
 ΔWarehouse
 i?:          ITEM
 qty?:        ℕ
 _____
 i? ∈ carried
 level' = level ⊕ {i? ↦ level i? + qty?}
 carried' = carried
```

Only deliveries for carried items are accepted. There is no upper limit on stock held.

```
__ CarryNewItem _____
 ΔWarehouse
 i?:          ITEM
 _____
 i? ∉ carried
 level' = level ∪ {i? ↦ 0}
 carried' = carried ∪ i?
```

A new item must not already be carried and will initially have a level of zero.

```
┌─── DiscontinueItem ────────
│ ΔWarehouse
│ i?:              ITEM
│├──────────────────────
│ i? ∈ carried
│ level i? = 0
│ carried' = carried \ i?
│ level' = i? ⊲ level
│
└────────────────────────
```

An item to be discontinued must currently be carried and must have a level of zero.

Note: errors have not been handled in this simple version.

Example from data processing

Indexed-sequential files

In the programming language COBOL a type of data file called an indexed-sequential file is available. In principle an indexed-sequential file is a sequence of records which can be accessed in any order by specifying the value of a field of the desired record, called the *key*. There is at most one record in the file for any value of the key.

Operations are available to read, write, insert and delete records (using the COBOL instructions READ, REWRITE, WRITE and DELETE respectively). The behaviour of these operations can be specified as follows:

[KEY]   set of all keys for this file

[DATA]   remaining fields of record (other than key)

```
┌─── ISFile ──────────
│ file:       KEY ⇸ DATA
│├──────────────────
│
└──────────────────
```

The file is regarded as a function from a key to the rest of the data in the record. The function is partial since there may be values of the key for which there is no record on the file.

Read operation

The operation *Read* is a function application:

```
┌─ Read ────────────────────
│ ΞISFile
│ k?:          KEY
│ result!:     DATA
├───────────────────
│ k? ∈ dom file
│ result! = file k?
└───────────────────────
```

The value of *result!* is the data of the record with the key *k?*, if there is one. The file is unchanged.

Rewrite operation

The operation *Rewrite* is a functional overriding:

```
┌─ Rewrite ────────────────
│ ΔISFile
│ k?:          KEY
│ new?:        DATA
├───────────────────
│ k? ∈ dom file
│ file' = file ⊕ {k? ↦ new?}
└───────────────────────
```

The function is changed only for the value of *k?* in the domain, which now maps to the new data *new?*.

Write operation

The operation *Write* is a functional (relational) union:

```
┌─ Write ────────────────
│ ΔISFile
│ k?:          KEY
│ new?:        DATA
├───────────────────
│ k? ∉ dom file
│ file' = file ∪ {k? ↦ new?}
└───────────────────────
```

Delete operation

The operation *Delete* is a functional (relational) domain anti-restriction:

```
___ Delete_____
 ΔISFile
 k?:              KEY
_____
 k? ∈ dom file
 file' = {k?} ⩤ file

_____
```

Error conditions

The handling of errors has not been included here, to keep the specification simple. The schemas could easily be extended to include a report of success or failure.

Further facilities

The COBOL language allows further operations on indexed-sequential files which make use of the fact that the records of such a file are held in order (ordered on the key). Clearly the specification used above would not suffice to specify those operations. However it gives a very concise explanation of the simple operations.

Summary of notation

$X \nrightarrow Y$ the set of partial functions from X to Y:
$== \{ f: X \leftrightarrow Y \mid (\forall x: X \mid x \in \text{dom } f \bullet$
$(\exists_1 y: Y \bullet x \, f \, y))\}$

$X \rightarrow Y$ the set of total functions from X to Y:
$== \{ f: X \nrightarrow Y \mid \text{dom } f = X \bullet f\}$

$f \, x \; or \; f(x)$ the function f applied to x

$f \oplus g$ functional overriding
$== (\text{dom } g \, ⩤ \, f) \cup g$

Exercises

A system records the bookings of hotel rooms on one night.

Given the basic types

        [ROOM]   the set of all the rooms in the hotel
        [PERSON]   the set of all possible persons

the state of the hotel's bookings can be represented by the following schema:

```
___ Hotel _____
  bookedTo:   ROOM ⇸ PERSON
|_____
```

10.1) Explain why *bookedTo* is a *function*.

10.2) Explain why the function is *partial*.

An initial state is:

```
___ Init _____
 Hotel
  _____
  bookedTo = ∅
|_____
```

and a first version of the operation to accept a booking is:

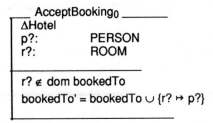

```
___ AcceptBooking₀ _____
 ΔHotel
 p?:         PERSON
 r?:         ROOM
 _____
 r? ∉ dom bookedTo
 bookedTo' = bookedTo ∪ {r? ↦ p?}
|_____
```

10.3) Explain the meaning and purpose of each line of the schema *AcceptBooking₀*.

10.4) Write a schema *CancelBooking₀* which cancels a booking made for a given person and a given room. It should deal with error conditions in the same manner as *AcceptBooking₀*.

10.5) Explain the meaning and purpose of each line of your schema *CancelBooking₀*.

11 A Seat Allocation System

Introduction

This example concerns recording the allocation of seats to passengers on an aircraft.

The types

The types involved here are the set of *all possible* persons, called *PERSON,* and the set of all seats *on this aircraft, SEAT.*

[PERSON]	the set of all possible uniquely identified persons
[SEAT]	the set of all seats on this aircraft

The state

The state of the system is given by the relation between the set of seats and the set of persons:

```
__ Seating_____
  | bookedTo:   SEAT ⇸ PERSON
  |_____
```

Note that a seat may be booked to only one person, but a person may book many seats.

Initial state

There must be an initial state for the system. The obvious one is the where the aircraft is entirely unbooked:

```
__Init_____
| Seating
|_____
| bookedTo = Ø
|
```

Operations

Booking

There is an operation to allow a person $p?$, to book the seat $s?$. A first attempt is:

```
__Book_0_____
| ΔSeating
| p?:        PERSON
| s?:        SEAT
|_____
| s? ∉ dom bookedTo
| bookedTo' = bookedTo ∪ {s? ↦ p?}
|
```

Cancel

It is also necessary to have an operation to allow a person $p?$ to cancel a booking for a seat $s?$:

```
__Cancel_0_____
| ΔSeating
| p?:        PERSON
| s?:        SEAT
|_____
| s? ↦ p? ∈ bookedTo
| bookedTo' = bookedTo \ { s? ↦ p?}
|
```

Enquiry operations

These operations leave the state unchanged.

Whose seat

In addition to operations which change the state of the system it is necessary to have an operation to discover the owner of a seat:

$$REPLY ::= yes \mid no$$

```
__ WhoseSeat ____________
ΞSeating
s?:          SEAT
taken!:      REPLY
who!:        PERSON
________________
(s? ∈ dom bookedTo ∧
taken! = yes ∧
who! = bookedTo s? )
∨
(s? ∉ dom bookedTo ∧
taken! = no)
________________
```

Dealing with errors

The schemas $Book_0$ and $Cancel_0$ do not state what happens if their preconditions are not satisfied. The schema calculus of Z allows these schemas to be extended, firstly to give a message in the event of success:

RESPONSE ::= OK | alreadyBooked | notYours

OKMessage ≙ [rep!: RESPONSE| rep! = OK]

Booking

A schema to handle errors on making a booking is defined:

```
__ BookError ____________
ΞSeating
s?:          SEAT
p?:          PERSON
rep!:        RESPONSE
________________
s? ∈ bookedTo
rep! = alreadyBooked
________________
```

Finally *Book* can be defined:

Book ≙ ($Book_0$ ∧ OKMessage) ∨ BookError

Cancel

A schema to handle errors on cancelling a booking is defined:

```
┌─ CancelError ──────────────
│ ΞSeating
│ s?:        SEAT
│ p?:        PERSON
│ repl:      RESPONSE
│ ──────────────────────────
│ s? ↦ p? ∉ bookedTo
│ repl = notYours
└───────────────────────────
```

Finally *Cancel* can be defined:

$$\text{Cancel} \triangleq (\text{Cancel}_0 \wedge \text{OKMessage}) \vee \text{CancelError}$$

Exercises

By using schema inclusion where possible, extend your specification of the computer system from exercise 2.1 and onwards to include security passwords. Each registered user must have a password. On being registered a user is given a dummy password. Use the declarations:

PASSWORD   the set of all possible passwords

dummy: PASSWORD

11.1) Give a schema to define the state of this system.

11.2) Give an initial state for the system.

11.3) Give a schema for the operation to register a new user.

11.4) Give a schema for the operation to log in. The user must give the correct password. Consider only the case where the user gives the correct password.

11.5) Give a schema for a logged-in user to change the password. The user must supply the new and the old passwords. Define only the case where the conditions are met.

12 Sequences

A sequence is a function

Very often it is necessary to be able to distinguish values of a set by position or to permit duplicate values or to impose some ordering on the values. For this a *sequence* is the appropriate structure.

A sequence of elements of type X is regarded in Z as a function from the natural numbers to elements of X. The domain of the function is defined to be the interval of the natural numbers starting from one and going up to the number of elements in the sequence, with no gaps.

A sequence s of elements of type X is declared:

   s: seq X

and is equivalent to declaring the function:

   $s: \mathbb{N} \twoheadrightarrow X$

with the constraint that:

   dom s = 1 .. #s

Sequence constructors

A sequence constant can be constructed by listing its elements in order, enclosed by special angle brackets and separated by commas:

[CITY]	the set of cities of the world
flight:	seq CITY

flight = ⟨ Geneva, Paris, London, New York ⟩

This is a shorthand for the function:

flight = { 1 ↦ Geneva, 2 ↦ Paris, 3 ↦ London, 4 ↦ New York}

The order of cities in *flight* might be the order in which those cities are visited on a journey starting in Geneva and finishing in New York.

The length of a sequence

The length of a sequence s is simply the size of the function

s

so

#flight = 4

Empty sequence

The sequence with no elements is written as empty sequence brackets:

⟨ ⟩

Non-empty sequences

If a sequence may never be empty, that is, it must always have at least one element, it can be declared:

s: seq_1 X

which is the same as defining

s: seq X

and adding the constraint

#s > 0

Sequence operators

Selection

Since a sequence is a function, it is possible to select an element by position simply by function application. For example to select the third element of *flight* :

> flight 3   this is London

As with a function, it only makes sense to attempt to select with a value which is in the domain of the function. In terms of the sequence, that means the position value must be between one and the number of elements in the sequence.

Head

The *head* of a sequence is its first element, so

> head flight

is the same as

> flight 1   this is Geneva

Tail

The *tail* of a sequence is the sequence with its head removed, so

> tail flight

is the sequence

> ⟨ London, Paris, New York ⟩

Last

The *last* of a sequence is its last element, so

> last flight

is the same as

flight #flight   this is New York

Front

The *front* of a sequence is the sequence with its last element removed, so

front flight

is the sequence

⟨ Geneva, Paris, London ⟩

Concatenation

The *concatenation* operator is written

and pronounced "concatenated with" or "catenated with". It chains to-gether two sequences to form a new sequence. For example:

⟨ Geneva, Paris, London, New York ⟩ ⁀ ⟨ Seattle, Tokyo ⟩

is the sequence

⟨ Geneva, Paris, London, New York, Seattle, Tokyo ⟩

Filtering

The operation called *filtering* a sequence produces a new sequence, all of whose elements are members of a specified set. Its effect is similar to that of performing a range restriction, then "squashing up" the elements to close up the gaps left by omitted elements. For example:

flight ↾ {London, Geneva, Rome}

is pronounced "flight filtered by the set containing London, Geneva and Rome" and results in the sequence:

⟨ Geneva, London ⟩

          Formal Specification Using Z

Note that the ordering remains that of the original sequence.
To form the sequence of those cities of *flight* which are in Europe:

flight ⇂ EuropeanCities

which is

⟨ Geneva, Paris, London⟩

given

EuropeanCities: ℙCITY
EuropeanCities = {Paris, London, Geneva, Rome}

Restriction and squash

Since a sequence is a function and a function is a relation, the relational
operators can be used. The relational restriction operators are particularly
useful; for example to select parts of a sequence.

Given:

S: seq X

then

1..n ◁ S

is the sequence of the first *n* elements of *S*.

In general a restriction of a sequence *does not* yield a *sequence*, since
the resulting domain will not be of contiguous natural numbers starting at
one. In that case the special operator *squash* can be used to convert the
relation into a sequence by "closing up the gaps".

So:

squash (m..n ◁ S)

is the *sequence* of the elements from position *m* to position *n* of *S*.
The sequence filtering

flight ⌐ EuropeanCities

is equivalent to

squash (flight ▷ EuropeanCities)

Reversing a sequence

The operator

rev

reverses the order of elements in a sequence. For example

rev flight = ⟨ New York, London, Paris, Geneva ⟩

Range

Since a sequence is just a special case of a function, it is permissible, and sometimes useful, to refer to the *range* of a sequence; that is, the *set* of values which appear in the sequence. For example:

ran flight = { Geneva, London, New York, Paris}

Example of using sequences – stack

The well known and widely used data structure called a *stack* can be defined by means of sequences.

A stack is a data structure into which elements can be added ("pushed") and removed ("popped"). The next element to be popped is the one most recently pushed. This behaviour is also explained by referring to this as a *last-in-first-out* structure.

Types

The general type X is used:

[X]   any type

The state

```
__ Stack _____
 s:              seq X
|_____
```

The initial state

```
__ Init _____
 Stack
|_____
 s = ⟨ ⟩
|_____
```

Initially the sequence *s* is empty.

Push

A new element will be added at the front of the sequence:

```
__ Push _____
 ΔStack
 x?:          X
|_____
 s' = ⟨x⟩ ⌢ s
|_____
```

Note that the new value could just as well have been added at the back of the sequence, so long as *Pop* then had the appropriate definition.

Pop

An element will be removed from the front of the sequence:

```
__ Pop _____
 ΔStack
 x!:          X
|_____
 s ≠ ⟨ ⟩
 x! = head s
 s' = tail s
|_____
```

The precondition of *Pop* is that the sequence *s* should not already be empty.

An alternative definition of *Pop*, which shows its symmetry with *Push*, is:

```
┌─ Pop ──────────────────
│ ΔStack
│ x!:          X
├────────────────────────
│ s ≠ ⟨ ⟩
│ s = ⟨ x! ⟩ ^ s'
└────────────────────────
```

Length

The *length* of the stack is the length of the sequence

```
┌─ Length ──────────────
│ ΞStack
│ len!:        N
├───────────────────────
│ len! = # s
└───────────────────────
```

A simple proof

An obvious property of a correct specification of the stack is that a *Push* immediately followed by a *Pop* should return the value *pushed* and leave the sequence unchanged. In other words, *Push* then *Pop* should be a *null* operation.

This is can be stated by proposing that the composition of *Push* with *Pop* should have the effect of popping the value pushed and leaving the stack unchanged:

```
┌─ Push ; Pop ──────────────
│ s:          seq X
│ s':         seq X
│ x?:         X
│ x!:         X
├───────────────────────────
│ x? = x!
│ s' = s
└───────────────────────────
```

This can be proved in the following way:

Push ; Pop ≙ (Push [inter / s'] ∧ Pop [inter / s]) \ inter

The outcoming *s'* of *Push* is renamed to *inter*; the incoming *s* of *Pop* is renamed to *inter*; then *inter* is hidden.

```
__ Push [ inter / s'] _____
s:              seq X
inter:          seq X
x?:             X
_____
inter = ⟨x?⟩ ^ s
```

```
__ Pop [ inter / s] _____
inter:          seq X
s':             seq X
x!:             X
_____
inter ≠ ⟨ ⟩
inter = ⟨x!⟩ ^ s'
```

(Push [inter / s'] ∧ Pop [inter / s]) \ inter ≜

```
__ Push ⨟ Pop _____
s:              seq X
s':             seq X
x?:             X
x!:             X
_____
∃ inter: seq X •
(inter = ⟨x?⟩ ^ s
inter ≠ ⟨ ⟩
inter = ⟨x!⟩ ^ s')
```

which can easily be simplified to the required result.

Example of using sequences – an air route

A route to be taken by a passenger on a journey by air can be described by the sequence of airports that the passenger will pass through. For the proposed journey to be viable, adjacent airports on the route must be connected by air services.

[AIRPORT]   the set of airports in the world

```
__ AirServices _____
  connected: AIRPORT ↔ AIRPORT
```

An operation to propose a viable route from the originating to the destination airport might be:

```
__ ProposeRoute _____
  ΞAirServices
  from?, to?:   AIRPORT
  route!:       seq AIRPORT
  _____
  head route! = from?
  last route! = to?
  (∀ changePos: N |
  changePos ∈ 1..#route! − 1 •
  route changePos connected
  route changePos + 1)
```

Of course there may in fact not be a viable route between any two airports.

Note that this operation does not rule out providing a route which goes through the same airport more than once, and even allows flights which land back where they started. Since it seems unlikely that passengers would wish to fly more legs on their journeys unnecessarily, a better version would eliminate such excessively long routes:

```
__ NoDuplicatesRoute ____
  ProposeRoute
  _____
  (∀ i, j: N |
  i ∈ 1..#route! ∧ j ∈ 1..#route! •
  i ≠ j ⇒ route i ≠ route j)
```

This says that for any i and j within the domain of the function (legal positions), if i and j are different, then so are the values in the sequence at positions i and j.

An alternative way of stating that no duplicates are permitted is to require that the inverse of the sequence be a function:

```
┌─ NoDuplicatesRoute ────
│ ProposeRoute
├────────────────────────
│ route˜ ∈ AIRPORT ⇸ N
│
└────────────────────────
```

Sequences with no duplicates permitted

To specify that there are to be no duplicates in a sequence is a common requirement and so, for convenience, a special declaration of an *injective* sequence can be used.

> iseq X

is the set of sequences of *X*'s where no value of *X* appears more than once in the sequence.

```
┌─── NoDuplicatesRoute ────
│ ΞAirServices
│ from?, to?:   AIRPORT
│ route!:        iseq AIRPORT
├──────────────────────────
│ head route! = from?
│ last route! = to?
│ (∀ changePos: N |
│ changePos ∈ 1..#route! − 1 •
│ route changePos connected
│ route changePos + 1)
│
└──────────────────────────
```

Example of using sequences – files in Pascal

In the programming language Pascal a file is a sequential structure of any type of elements. A file can be either in *inspection* mode or in *generation* mode. The file is put into inspection mode by a *Reset* operation and when in inspection mode can be read from by a *Read* operation. The file is put into *generation* mode by a *Rewrite* operation which makes the file empty. When in *generation* mode the file can have new elements appended to it by a *Write* operation.

This specification ignores buffering of data.

> [X]   any type of data (some restrictions in Pascal)
> FILEMODE ::= inspection | generation

The file state

```
 ___PascalFile_____
| file:         seq X
| stillToRead:  seq X
| mode:         FILEMODE
|_____
| ∃ alreadyRead: seq X •
| alreadyRead ⁀ stillToRead = file
|_____
```

the part of the file still to be read is always a *suffix* of the whole file.

The Reset operation

```
 ___Reset_____
| ΔPascalFile
|_____
| mode' = inspection
| stillToRead' = file
| file' = file
|_____
```

The mode is switched to inspection and the whole of the file is still to be read. The content of the file is not changed by this operation.

The Read operation

```
 ___Read_____
| ΔPascalFile
| x!:           X
|_____
| mode = inspection
| stillToRead ≠ ⟨ ⟩
| ⟨ x! ⟩ ⁀ stillToRead' = stillToRead
| file' = file
| mode' = mode
|_____
```

The mode must be inspection; the part of the file still to be read must not be empty. The value returned is taken from the front of the part of the file still to be read. The file and its mode are unchanged.

The Rewrite operation

```
┌─ Rewrite ──────────────
│ ΔPascalFile
│ ─────────────────────
│ mode' = generation
│ file' = ⟨ ⟩
│
└────────────────────────
```

The mode is switched to generation and the file becomes empty.

The Write operation

```
┌─ Write ────────────────
│ ΔPascalFile
│ x?:              X
│ ─────────────────────
│ mode = generation
│ file' = file ⌢ ⟨ x? ⟩
│ mode' = mode
│
└────────────────────────
```

The mode must be generation. The value to be written is appended to the file. The mode is unchanged.

End of file

End of file is true when the part of the file still to be read is an empty sequence

$$\text{stillToRead} = \langle \, \rangle$$

Summary of notation

seq X	the set of sequences whose elements are drawn from X
	$== \{S: \, \mathbb{N} \nrightarrow X \mid \text{dom } S = 1 \, .. \, \#S\}$
seq$_1$ X	set of non-empty sequences
iseq X	set of injective sequences (no duplicates)

#S	the length of the sequence S
$\langle\,\rangle$	the empty sequence { }
$\langle x_1, \dots x_n \rangle$	$== \{\, 1 \mapsto x_1, \dots, n \mapsto x_n \}$
$\langle x_1, \dots x_n \rangle ^\smallfrown \langle y_1, \dots y_n \rangle$	
	concatenation:
	$== \langle x_1, \dots x_n, y_1, \dots y_n \rangle$

head S	$== S\ 1$
last S	$== S\ \#S$
tail $\langle x \rangle ^\smallfrown S$	$== S$
front $S ^\smallfrown \langle x \rangle$	$== S$

squash f	the function f squashed into a sequence
S $\upharpoonright$ s	the sequence S filtered to elements in s
	$==$ squash (S $\rhd$ s)
rev S	the sequence S in reverse order

Exercises

12.1) Given the sequences of cities:

    u, v: seq CITY

and the values

    u = $\langle$ London, Amsterdam, Madrid $\rangle$

and

    v = $\langle$ Paris, Frankfurt $\rangle$

write down the values of the sequences:

    u $^\smallfrown$ v
    rev (u $^\smallfrown$ v)
    rev u
    rev v
    rev v $^\smallfrown$ rev u

Referring to 12.1:

12.2) find the value of

squash (2 .. 4 ◁ rev (u ^ v))

12.3) find the value of

squash (4 .. 2 ◁ rev (u ^ v))

12.4) find the value of

u ^ v ▷ { London, Moscow, Paris, Rome }

12.5) find the value of

tail (u ^ v) ^ front ⟨ Moscow, Berlin, Warsaw ⟩

13 An example of sequences – the aircraft example again

Introduction

A system can be specified in terms of sequences. This chapter shows the aircraft example done in this fashion. Usually it is harder to use sequences; they are much less abstract than sets since order must be taken into account. A process called *refinement* concerns producing a more concrete specification from an abstract one. In so doing each transformation can be shown to be a correct implementation of its (more abstract) specification.

The state

The passengers' identifications are held in a sequence, which does not contain any name more than once:

```
┌─ SeqAircraft ─────────────
│ passengers: seq PERSON
├───────────────────────────
│ #passengers ≤ capacity
│ (∀ i, j: PERSON |
│ i ∈ dom passengers ∧ j ∈ dom passengers •
│ i ≠ j ⇒ passengers i ≠ passengers j )
└───────────────────────────
```

The relationship (the *abstraction function, ABS*) between the abstract specification *Aircraft* and the more concrete *SeqAircraft* is given by:

115

```
┌─ ABS ──────────────────
│ Aircraft
│ SeqAircraft
│ ─────────────────────
│ onboard = ran passengers
│
```

Initial state

The sequence is empty:

```
┌─ SeqInit ──────────────
│ SeqAircraft
│ ─────────────────────
│ passengers = ⟨ ⟩
│
```

Operations

Boarding

The new person is appended to (the end of) the sequence:

```
┌─ SeqBoard──────────────
│ p?:            PERSON
│ ΔSeqAircraft
│ ─────────────────────
│ p? ∉ ran passengers
│ #passengers < capacity
│ passengers' = passengers ⌢ ⟨p?⟩
│
```

Disembark

```
┌─ SeqDisembark ─────────
│ p?:            PERSON
│ ΔSeqAircraft
│ ─────────────────────
│ p? ∈ ran passengers
│ ( ∃ before, after: seq PERSON •
│     passengers = before ⌢ ⟨p?⟩ ⌢ after ∧
│     passengers' = before ⌢ after )
│
```

Note how much more complex this is than the set-based version; the element must be removed from the right place in the sequence.

Enquiry operations

Number on board

```
___ SeqNumber _____
numOnBoard!:      N
ΞSeqAircraft
_____
numonboard! = #passengers
```

The number on board is the length of the sequence, since there are no duplicates.

Person on board

REPLY ::= yes | no

```
___ SeqOnBoard _____
p?:            PERSON
rep!:          REPLY
ΞSeqAircraft
_____
(p? ∈ ran passengers ∧
rep = yes)

∨

(p? ∉ ran passengers ∧
rep = no)
```

Dealing with errors

For the sake of simplicity the sections on dealing with errors have been omitted here.

Implementation

Since a sequence is easily modelled in a programming language, either by the language's sequence type in the case of an applicative language, or by files or arrays in a procedural language, a sequence is closer to being implementable than, say, a set or a relation, and is thus regarded as being more concrete. In a complex specification it is best to start with a simpler, more abstract specification, in terms of sets, functions and so on, and to refine this later to a more concrete, equivalent specification. This process of refinement is itself the subject of books.

Exercises

13.1) Define a schema for the state of a system which will maintain a *file* which is a sequence of *bytes*.

13.2) Give a schema for a suitable initial state of the file.

13.3) Give a schema for an operation to *insert* a sequence of bytes *after* a given position in the file.

13.4) Give a schema to *delete* the sequence of bytes within the file, given suitable starting and ending positions.

13.5) Give a schema to *copy* a sequence of bytes within the file, given the starting and ending positions, into an output *buffer*.

14   Extending a specification

Limitations of specifications given so far

The most complex specification given so far in this book concerns booking of seats on an aircraft. This example is unrealistic in that it only considers one flight of one aircraft. It is wise to start a specification in this way by simplifying the problem, but naturally it would be useful to extend this specification to consider many flights.

The type of a flight

The new type *FLIGHT* will be introduced for this extended specification.

      [FLIGHT]   the set of all flight identifications

If the flight identification is composed of a date and a flight number it could be declared as:

      [DATE]   the set of all dates
      [FLIGHTNO]   the set of all flight numbers

$$FLIGHT == DATE \times FLIGHTNO$$

The twin equal signs mean equivalence for types.

A function to a function

The behaviour of the extended system of seat allocations across a fleet of aircraft is to be the same for each flight, so the new seat allocation information can conveniently be represented by a function from flight to seat allocation for that flight. The seat allocation for a flight will be, as before, a function from seat to person.

> [SEAT]   the set of all seats in all aircraft
> [PERSON]   the set of all persons

The state schema will use the function *allocation*:

> allocation: FLIGHT $\nrightarrow$ (SEAT $\nrightarrow$ PERSON)

Note that for any flight f

> allocation f

is a function from *SEAT* to *PERSON*, as in the previous, simpler version of this specification, and, for any seat s

> allocation f s

is the application of the function from *SEAT* to *PERSON* yielded by the application of the function *allocation* to the flight f, and is thus the person to whom the seat s on flight f is booked.

Flights

Since it is necessary to know about which flights exist, the set *knownFlights* is introduced. It holds the designations of all flights handled by this system. Seat allocations are only permitted for known flights.

Seats and aircraft

It is no longer sufficient to consider the set *SEAT* to be the set of seats on this aircraft, since there are now several aircraft involved. For this reason *SEAT* has been declared as the set of all seats in all aircraft and a new function *hasSeat* is used to discover what seats a flight has assigned to it.

The relating of a seat to a flight rather than to a particular aircraft reflects the fact that the same seat on a given aircraft can be booked many times in its lifetime, but only once for a given flight of that aircraft.

The state

Seats may only be allocated on known flights and only the seats assigned to a flight may be booked.

```
____ FleetSeatAllocation _____
allocation:    FLIGHT ⇸ (SEAT ⇸ PERSON)
hasSeat:       FLIGHT ↔ SEAT
knownFlights:       ℙFLIGHT
_____
dom allocation ⊆ knownFlights
∀ f: FLIGHT •
dom allocation f ⊆ hasSeat (| {f} |)
```

allocation

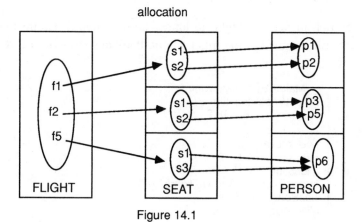

Figure 14.1

Initial state

A possible initial state is where there are no bookings for any seats on any flights.

```
____ Init _____
FleetSeatAllocation
_____
hasSeat = ∅
allocation = ∅
knownFlights = ∅
```

Operations

Making a flight known

An operation to make a flight known is

```
┌─ MakeFlightKnown₀ ──────
│ ΔFleetSeatAllocation
│ f?:            FLIGHT
├──────────────────────
│ f? ∉ knownFlights
│ knownFlights' = knownFlights ∪ {f?}
│ hasSeat' = hasSeat
│ allocation' = allocation ∪ {f? ↦ ∅}
│
└──────────────────────
```

The flight must not already be known.

Making a flight unknown

An operation to make a flight no longer known should require that no seats are still assigned to the flight and no bookings are still in force for the flight.

```
┌─ MakeFlightUnknown₀ ──
│ ΔFleetSeatAllocation
│ f?:            FLIGHT
├──────────────────────
│ f? ∈ knownFlights
│ hasSeat ⦇ {f?} ⦈ = ∅
│ allocation f? = ∅
│ knownFlights' = knownFlights \ {f?}
│ hasSeat' = hasSeat
│ allocation' = allocation
│
└──────────────────────
```

Assigning a seat to a flight

An operation to assign a seat to a flight is

```
___ Assign₀ _____
ΔFleetSeatAllocation
f?:            FLIGHT
s?:            SEAT
_____
f? ∈ knownFlights
¬ f? hasSeat s?
hasSeat' = hasSeat ∪ {f? ↦ s?}
knownFlights' = knownFlights
allocation' = allocation
_____
```

The flight must be known and the seat must not already be assigned to a flight.

Removing the assignment of a seat to a flight

An operation to remove the assignment of a seat to a flight is

```
___ DeAssign₀ _____
ΔFleetSeatAllocation
f?:            FLIGHT
s?:            SEAT
_____
f? ∈ knownFlights
f? hasSeat s?
hasSeat' = hasSeat \ {f? ↦ s?}
knownFlights' = knownFlights
allocation' = allocation
_____
```

The flight must be known and the seat must already be assigned to the flight.

Booking a seat on a flight

An operation to book a seat on a particular flight needs to have flight, seat and person as input.

```
┌─ Book₀ ─────────────────────
│ ΔFleetSeatAllocation
│ f?:          FLIGHT
│ s?:          SEAT
│ p?:          PERSON
├─────────────────────────────
│ f? ∈ knownFlights
│ f? ∈ dom allocation
│ f? hasSeat s?
│ s? ∉ dom allocation f?
│ allocation' = allocation ⊕ {f? ↦ allocation f? ∪ {s? ↦ p?} }
│ knownFlights' = knownFlights
│ hasSeat' = hasSeat
└─────────────────────────────
```

The flight must be known, the seat must be assigned to this flight and the seat must not already be booked.

Cancelling a booking

An operation to cancel a booking needs to have flight, seat and person as input.

```
┌─ Cancel₀ ───────────────────
│ ΔFleetSeatAllocation
│ f?:          FLIGHT
│ s?:          SEAT
│ p?:          PERSON
├─────────────────────────────
│ f? ∈ knownFlights
│ f? ∈ dom allocation
│ f? hasSeat s?
│ s? ↦ p? ∈ allocation f?
│ knownFlights' = knownFlights
│ allocation' = allocation ⊕ {f? ↦ allocation f? \ {s? ↦ p?} }
│ hasSeat' = hasSeat
└─────────────────────────────
```

The flight must be known, the seat must be assigned to this flight and the seat must be booked to the person.

Enquiry operations

Enquiry about a booking

An operation to enquire about a booking needs to have flight and seat as input:

REPLY ::= yes | no

```
__ Enquire _____
ΞFleetSeatAllocation
f?:          FLIGHT
s?:          SEAT
taken!:      REPLY
who!:        PERSON
_____
f? ∈ knownFlights
f? ∈ dom allocation
f? hasSeat s?
(s? ∈ dom allocation f? ∧ taken! = yes ∧ who! = allocation f? s?)
∨
(s? ∉ dom allocation f? ∧ taken! = no)
```

The flight must be known and the seat must be assigned to this flight.

Error conditions

This extended example has made preconditions of operations explicit. Error handling schemas can be defined to handle the violation of preconditions by returning a result value, as in previous examples. This part has been omitted here since it introduces no new ideas.

Conclusions

This more realistic specification is much more complex than the earlier examples and is nonetheless for a fairly modest system. It is wise to specify a simple version of any problem first, before taking on the entire complexity of any problem.

Exercises

A company lets its apartments to known customers for fixed time-slots. At any given time an apartment may only be booked to one person. A system is required to handle bookings. From time to time apartments are acquired and given up.

For a formal specification of this system give the following:

14.1) Schemas to describe the state of the system and an initial state.

14.2) A schema for the operation to record a new customer.

14.3) A schema for the operation to acquire a new apartment.

14.4) A schema for the operation to make a booking of an apartment to a given customer at a given time.

14.5) A schema for an enquiry operation to show all apartments which are free at a given time.

Appendix 1 Collected notation

General

[X]   the basic type X

data type ::= member$_1$ | member$_2$ | ... | member$_n$

X == Y   abbreviation definition – X stands for Y

Sets

Z   the set of integers (whole numbers)

N   the set of natural numbers (≥ 0)

N$_1$ the set of positive natural numbers (≥ 1)

$t \in S$ t is an element of S

$t \notin S$ t is not an element of S

$S \subseteq T$ S is contained in T.

$S \subset T$ S is strictly contained in T. ($S \neq T$)

$\emptyset$ or { } the empty set

$\{t_1, t_2, ... t_n\}$ the set containing $t_1, t_2, ... t_n$

PS   Powerset: the set of all subsets of S

FS   the set of finite subsets of S

$S \cup T$ Union: elements that are either in S or T

$S \cap T$ Intersection: elements that are both in S and in T

$S \setminus T$ Difference: elements that are in S but not in T

#S   Size: number of elements in S

$\{D \mid P \bullet t\}$ the set of t's such that given declarations D, P holds

m .. n   the set of numbers m to n inclusive

$\bigcup$ SS   the distributed union of the set of sets SS

$\cap$ SS	the distributed intersection of the set of sets SS
disjoint sqs	the sets in the sequence sqs are disjoint
sqs partition S	the sets in sqs partition the set S

Logic

true, false	logical constants
$\neg$ P	negation: "not P"
P $\wedge$ Q	conjunction: "P and Q"
P $\vee$ Q	disjunction: "P or Q"
P $\Rightarrow$ Q	implication: "P implies Q" or "if P then Q"
P $\Leftrightarrow$ Q	equivalence: "P is logically equivalent to Q"
t1 = t2	equality between terms
$t_1 \neq t_2$	$\neg(t_1 = t_2)$

Schemas

S $\hat{=}$ T   schema definition: S is the same schema as T

```
___ SchemaName _____
| declarations
|_____
| predicate
|_____
```

SchemaName $\hat{=}$ [declarations | predicate]

Axiomatic definition

```
| declarations
|_____
| predicate
```

The following examples use

S $\hat{=}$ [a, b: N | a < b]

Inclusion

```
__ IncludeS _____
| c:            N
| S
|_____
| c < 10
|_____
```

≙

```
__ IncludeS _____
| c:            N
| a, b:         N
|_____
| c < 10
| a < b
|_____
```

Conjunction

```
__ T _____
| b, c:         N
|_____
| b < c
|_____
```

SandT ≙ S ∧ T

≙

```
__ SandT _____
| a, b, c:      N
|_____
| a < b
| b < c
|_____
```

Disjunction

SorT ≙ S ∨ T

≙

```
__ SorT _____
| a, b, c:      N
|_____
| a < b ∨ b < c
|_____
```

Implication

SimpIT ≜ S ⇒ T

≜

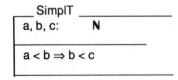

```
┌─ SimpIT ─────────────
│ a, b, c:      N
│ ─────────────────────
│ a < b ⇒ b < c
└──────────────────────
```

Equivalence

SeqT ≜ S ⇔ T

≜

```
┌─ SeqT ─────────────
│ a, b, c:      N
│ ─────────────────────
│ a < b ⇔ b < c
└──────────────────────
```

Decoration

```
┌─ S ─────────────
│ a, b:      N
│ ─────────────────────
│ a < b
└──────────────────────
```

```
┌─ S' ─────────────
│ a', b':      N
│ ─────────────────────
│ a' < b'
└──────────────────────
```

Predicates and their use with schemas

∀ x: T • P_x Universal quantification:
                                      "for all x of type T, P_x holds"

∃ x: T • P_x Existential quantification:
                                        "there exists an x of type T, where P_x holds"

$\exists_1 x: T \cdot P_x$ Unique existence:

"there exists a unique x of type T, such that P_x holds"

$$== (\exists x: T \cdot P_x \wedge \neg (\exists y: T \mid x \neq y \cdot P_y))$$

S[new / old,...]	schema renaming
$S \setminus (x_1, x_2, ... x_n)$	schema hiding
$S \upharpoonright (x_1, x_2, ... x_n)$	schema projection
pre S	precondition of S
S $\stackrel{\circ}{,}$ T	schema composition: S, then T

Relations

$X \times Y$	the set of ordered pairs of X's and Y's
$X \leftrightarrow Y$	the set of relations from X to Y: $== \mathbb{P}(X \times Y)$
x R y	x is related by R to y: $== (x, y) \in R$
$x \mapsto y$	$== (x, y)$
$\{ x_1 \mapsto y_1, x_2 \mapsto y_2, ..., x_n \mapsto y_n \}$	

$== $ the relation $\{ (x_1, y_1), (x_2, y_2), ..., (x_n, y_n) \}$

relating x_1 to y_1, x_2 to y_2, ..., x_n to y_n

dom R	the domain of a relation
	$== \{x: X \mid (\exists y: Y . x R y) \cdot x\}$
ran R	the range of a relation
	$== \{y: Y \mid (\exists x: X . x R y) \cdot y\}$

R (S)	the relational image of S in R
$S \triangleleft R$	the relation R domain restricted to S
$R \triangleright S$	the relation R range restricted to S
$S \ntriangleleft R$	the relation R domain anti-restricted to S
$R \ntriangleright S$	the relation R range anti-restricted to S
R ; Q	the forward composition of R with Q
$Q \circ R$	the backward composition of Q with R
R^+	the repeated self-composition of R
R^*	the repeated self-composition of R
	$== R^+ \cup \text{id } X$

id X	$\{x: X \bullet x \mapsto x\}$
R~	the inverse of R

Functions

$X \nrightarrow Y$	the set of partial functions from X to Y: $== \{ f: X \leftrightarrow Y \mid (\forall x: X \mid x \in \text{dom } f \bullet$ $(\exists_1 y: Y \bullet x\, f\, y))\}$
$X \rightarrow Y$	the set of total functions from X to Y: $== \{ f: X \nrightarrow Y \mid \text{dom } f = X \bullet f\}$
f x *or* f(x)	the function f applied to x
$f \oplus g$	functional overriding $== (\text{dom } g \mathbin{\vartriangleleft\mkern-10mu-} f) \cup g$

Sequences

seq X	the set of sequences whose elements are drawn from X $== \{S: \mathbf{N} \nrightarrow X \mid \text{dom } S = 1 .. \#S\}$
seq$_1$ X	set of non-empty sequences
iseq X	set of injective sequences (no duplicates)
#S	the length of the sequence S
$\langle\,\rangle$	the empty sequence { }
$\langle x_1, \dots x_n \rangle$	$== \{ 1 \mapsto x_1, \dots, n \mapsto x_n\}$
$\langle x_1, \dots x_n \rangle \,^\frown\, \langle y_1, \dots y_n \rangle$	
	concatenation: $== \langle x_1, \dots x_n , y_1, \dots y_n \rangle$
head S	$== S\, 1$
last S	$== S\, \#S$

tail ⟨ x ⟩ ^ S   == S
front S ^ ⟨ x ⟩   == S

squash f   the function f squashed into a sequence
S ↾ s   the sequence S filtered to those elements in s
                       == squash (S ▷ s)
rev S   the sequence S in reverse order

Appendix 2
Books on formal specification

Specification Case Studies, I. Hayes (ed), Prentice-Hall, 1987

A series of tutorial papers on Z. Notation a little out of date in places now, but this should not cause any difficulties of understanding.

The Z Notation: A Reference Manual, J. M. Spivey, Prentice-Hall, 1989

Currently the reference manual for Z. Not intended as a tutorial but does have a good tutorial introduction.

Introduction to Discrete Mathematics for Software Engineering, T. Denvir, Macmillan, 1986

Includes the mathematics of formal specification.

Software Engineering Mathematics: Formal Methods Demystified, J. Woodcock and M. Loomes, Pitman, 1988

Includes the mathematics needed for formal specification.

Understanding Z: A Specification Language and its Formal Semantics, J. M. Spivey, Cambridge University Press, 1988

The mathematical basis of Z.

An Introduction to Discrete Mathematics and Formal Systems Specification, Darrel Ince, Oxford Applied Mathematics and Computer Science Series, Oxford University Press, 1988

A thorough coverage of the material.

Appendix 3
Hints on creating
specifications

Introduction

The process of creating formal specifications needs more than fluency with the mathematical tools provided by the Z notation. It requires imagination and investigation and the ability to revise one's work when difficulties arise and when a new approach offers itself. It has been said that the most important aid to formal specification is a large waste-paper basket!

This appendix offers some hints on how to go about creating formal specifications.

Types

Find out what the sets (types) in the system to be specified are. Keep these sets general. The style which uses "the set of all ..." allows you to consider a subset and to add new elements from the "set of all" to the subset and to remove elements from the subset.

For example: If you declare

[STUDENT]   the set of students at this Polytechnic

you cannot enrol any new students or allow students to leave, since the type is fixed.

The following is far better:

[PERSON]   the set of all persons

<pre>students: ℙPERSON</pre>

Be sure that your types are truly *atomic*: For example, don't declare a type *CLASS* meaning a *group of* students. Instead use the type *PERSON* as above and make *class* a subset.

Relationships

Next consider the relationships between the types. By discovering how many values of what type are related to how many of the other type, find out if any of the *relations* are *functions*. If so, are the functions *total* or *partial*, or *injective*? Are there any relationships between the relations and functions you have found? For example, must they have the same domains or must the domain of one contain the range of another?

If there is a natural order to some values, then think of using a sequence; otherwise it is easier to work with sets.

Remember that it is necessary to state the obvious!

The state

This investigation of relationships will lead to a schema which represents the *state*. You will also have discovered some *invariants*, which are included in the state schema.

Initial state

An *initial* state should be as simple as possible. Often it gives empty sets and relationships as the starting point. It is important that the initial state should not violate any invariant of the system. Ideally this will be *formally proved*. With a simple initial state it is usually easy to see that the invariants are not violated.

Operations

Start by considering the behaviour of each operation only when it is given sensible values. Include a check that the values are reasonable (the *precondition*), but do not deal with errors at this stage. At a later stage define a separate schema to deal with errors by returning a reply value.

Don't forget to state explicitly what does *not* change as a result of an operation.

Enquiry operations

Enquiry operations do not *change* the state, and thus cannot violate an invariant. Use a *xi* (Ξ) schema where possible.

In case of severe difficulty

If the specification is getting too hard, try viewing it in a more *abstract* way. Hide some of the details for now and try to take a broader view. Put the detail back in later when you have a better understanding of what you are trying to do.

Reading specifications

You can learn a lot by reading specifications. There are several in this book and also in books mentioned in appendix 2. Watch out in the journals for articles which include formal specifications.

Good luck!

Appendix 4
Solutions to exercises

Chapter 1

1.1)
- Monday – clearly the Friday is the 27th.
- Sunday – the whole weekend, so Friday = 28th.
- Saturday – is the weekend beginning 29th in September or not? It starts in September but ends on 1st October. Perhaps the event starts on the 22nd?
- Friday – is Friday part of a weekend. Does the event start on the 30th or on the 23rd?

A better specification would be, for example: "The event takes place on the weekend which includes the last Sunday in September".

1.2) First ambiguity: What does "next" Wednesday mean, when you are reading on a Monday – Wednesday 6th or Wednesday of next week, 13th?

Second ambiguity: Does on leave until Wednesday mean that the software engineer's last day of leave is Wednesday, or does it mean that the software engineer will be back on Wednesday?

The colleague might reasonably expect the software engineer next to be back at work on any of: Wednesday 6th, Thursday 7th, Wednesday 13th or Thursday 14th.

1.3) Some of these questions are answered by user handbooks, several are not. Answers from a particular user manual:
- invalid dates such as 31st April, day number not accepted.

• 29th February – question not dealt with by handbook, but since recorder does not store year it cannot know if 29th February exists or not.

• overlapping requests – not dealt with by handbook.

• New Year's Eve – not mentioned, but no problem.

• ordering of requests – not mentioned, but order does not matter.

1.4) You can't tell, but it matters a lot. (This was a real specification!)

1.5) *No answer.*

Chapter 2

2.1

```
[PERSON]     the set of all uniquely identifiable persons
users, loggedIn: PPERSON
loggedIn ⊆ users
```

2.2

```
limit: N
limit ∈ 32 .. 128
# loggedIn ≤ limit
```

2.3 Add:

```
staff, customers: PPERSON
```

and

```
staff ∩ customers = Ø
staff ∪ customers = users
```

or

```
⟨staff, customers⟩ partition users
```

2.4

```
loggedIn ⊆ staff
```

#customer > # staff

2.5)

$$\#loggedIn \leq \# users$$

is true. It is a consequence of:

$$loggedIn \subseteq users$$

Chapter 3

3.1) Invariant property. Only registered users can ever be logged-in.

$$loggedIn \subseteq users$$

3.2) Initial state: no users, no-one logged in. This satisfies the invariant.

$$users = \varnothing$$
$$loggedIn = \varnothing$$

3.3) Add new user. Person *p* must not already be a user. Person *p* is added to *users*.

p: PERSON

$$p \notin users$$
$$users' = users \cup \{p\}$$
$$loggedIn' = loggedIn$$

3.4) Remove user. Person *p* must already be a user. Person *p* is removed from *users*.

p: PERSON

$$p \in users$$
$$p \notin loggedIn$$

```
users' = users \ {p}
loggedIn' = loggedIn
```

3.5) Log in:

```
p ∈ users
p ∉ loggedIn
loggedIn' = loggedIn ∪ {p}
users' = users
```

Log out:

```
p ∈ users
p ∈ loggedIn
loggedIn' = loggedIn \ {p}
users' = users
```

Chapter 4

4.1) Law about implication

P	Q	$P \Rightarrow Q$
false	false	true
false	true	true
true	false	false
true	true	true

P	Q	$\neg P$	$\neg P \vee Q$	$P \Rightarrow Q \Leftrightarrow \neg P \vee Q$
false	false	true	true	true
false	true	true	true	true
true	false	false	false	true
true	true	false	true	true

4.2)

P	Q	$P \Rightarrow Q$	$Q \Rightarrow P$
false	false	true	true
false	true	true	false
true	false	false	true
true	true	true	true

$P \Rightarrow Q \wedge Q \Rightarrow P$	$P \Leftrightarrow Q$
true	true
false	false
false	false
true	true

4.3)

$\neg(p \notin \text{onboard} \wedge \#\text{onboard} < \text{capacity})$

$\Leftrightarrow$

$\neg(p \notin \text{onboard}) \vee \neg(\#\text{onboard} < \text{capacity})$

$\Leftrightarrow$

$p \in \text{onboard} \vee \#\text{onboard} \geq \text{capacity}$

4.4)

$(a \wedge b) \vee (a \wedge c) \vee (a \wedge \neg c)$

$\Leftrightarrow a \wedge (b \vee c \vee \neg c)$

$\Leftrightarrow a \wedge (b \vee \text{true})$

$\Leftrightarrow a \wedge \text{true}$

$\Leftrightarrow a$

4.5) The only way in which

$$p \in \text{loggedIn} \land p \in \text{user}$$

can be true is if both

$$p \in \text{loggedIn}$$

and

$$p \in \text{user}$$

are true. But, because of the given implication, if

$$p \in \text{loggedIn}$$

is true, then so is

$$p \in \text{user}$$

Chapter 5

5.1)

```
RESPONSE ::=
OK | AlreadyAUser | NotAUser | LoggedIn | NotLoggedIn
```

5.2) Add new user:

```
p: PERSON
reply: RESPONSE

loggedIn' = loggedIn
∧
((p ∉ users ∧
users' = users ∪ {p} ∧
reply = OK)
∨
```

$(p \in$ users $\wedge$
users' = users $\wedge$
reply = AlreadyAUser))

5.3) Remove user. This answer makes use of the invariant of this system:

loggedIn $\subseteq$ users

which implies that

$p \notin$ users $\Rightarrow p \notin$ loggedIn

p: PERSON
reply: RESPONSE

loggedIn' = loggedIn
$\wedge$
$((p \in$ users $\wedge$ p $\notin$ loggedIn $\wedge$
users' = users \ {p} $\wedge$ reply = OK)
$\vee$
$(p \notin$ users $\wedge$
users' = users $\wedge$ reply = NotAUser)
$\vee$
$(p \in$ users $\wedge$ p $\in$ loggedIn $\wedge$
users' = users $\wedge$ reply = LoggedIn))

5.4) Log in:

p: PERSON
reply: RESPONSE

users' = users
$\wedge$
$((p \in$ users $\wedge$ p $\notin$ loggedIn $\wedge$
loggedIn' = loggedIn $\cup$ {p} $\wedge$ reply = OK)
$\vee$
$(p \notin$ users $\wedge$

loggedIn' = loggedIn ∧ reply = NotAUser)

∨

(p ∈ users ∧ p ∈ loggedIn ∧

loggedIn' = loggedIn ∧ reply = LoggedIn))

5.5) Log out:

p: PERSON

reply: RESPONSE

users' = users

∧

((p ∈ users ∧ p ∈ loggedIn ∧

loggedIn' = loggedIn \ {p} ∧ reply = OK)

∨

(p ∉ users ∧

loggedIn' = loggedIn ∧ reply = NotAUser)

∨

(p ∈ users ∧ p ∉ loggedIn ∧

loggedIn' = loggedIn ∧ reply = NotLoggedIn))

Chapter 6

6.1) *LinesRemaining*

```
___ LinesRemaining _____
ΞCursor
lines!:        N
_____
lines! = numLines − line

```

or

```
___ LinesRemaining _____
ΔCursor
lines!:        N
_____
lines! = numLines − line
line' = line
column' = column

```

6.2) *UpKey*

This schema deals with what happens when the cursor is not on the top line of the display:

```
__UpKeyNormal _____
ΔCursor
key?:          KEY
_____
key? = up
line > 1
line' = line − 1
column' = column
```

The next schema deals with what happens when the cursor is on the top line of the display:

```
__UpKeyAtTop _____
ΔCursor
key?:          KEY
_____
key? = up
line = 1
line' = numLines
column' = column
```

Note that the cursor has been defined to *wrap round* to the bottom line of the display.

The full behaviour is given by:

$$UpKey \triangleq UpKeyNormal \lor UpKeyAtTop$$

6.3) *LeftKey*

The operation for moving left is given. It is easiest to deal first with what happens when the cursor is not at the far left of the display:

```
__LeftKeyNormal _____
ΔCursor
key?:          KEY
_____
key? = left
column > 1
column' = column − 1
line' = line
```

The next schema deals with the cursor's being at the left of a line other than the top line of the display. Note that the cursor wraps round to the start of the previous line:

```
┌─── LeftKeyAtStart ──────────
│ ΔCursor
│ key?:          KEY
├─────────────────────────
│ key? = left
│ column = 1
│ column' = numColumns
│ line > 1
│ line' = line − 1
│
└─────────────────────────
```

Finally, a separate schema deals with the cursor's being at the left of the top line. The cursor wraps round to the right of the bottom line:

```
┌─── LeftKeyAtTop ──────────
│ ΔCursor
│ key?:          KEY
├─────────────────────────
│ key? = left
│ column = 1
│ column' = numColumns
│ line = 1
│ line' = numLines
│
└─────────────────────────
```

These schemas can be combined to form one schema which defines the response of the cursor to a left-move key in all initial positions of the cursor.

$$LeftKey \triangleq LeftKeyNormal \lor LeftKeyAtStart \lor LeftKeyAtTop$$

6.4) *NewDownKey*

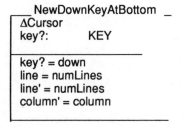

```
┌─── NewDownKeyAtBottom ──
│ ΔCursor
│ key?:          KEY
├─────────────────────────
│ key? = down
│ line = numLines
│ line' = numLines
│ column' = column
│
└─────────────────────────
```

$$NewDownKey \triangleq DownKeyNormal \lor NewDownKeyAtBottom$$

6.5) *NewRightKey*

```
___ NewRightKeyAtRight ___
ΔCursor
key?:          KEY
─────────────────────
key? = right
column = numColumns
column' = numcolumns
line' = line

```

NewRightKey ≜ RightKeyNormal ∨ NewRightKeyAtRight

Chapter 7

7.1)

[PERSON]   the set of all uniquely identifiable persons

```
___ Computer _____
users, loggedIn: ℙPERSON
────────────────────
loggedIn ⊆ users

```

```
___ InitComputer _____
Computer
────────────────
loggedIn = ∅
users = ∅

```

RESPONSE ::=
OK | AlreadyAUser | NotAUser | LoggedIn | NotLoggedIn

7.2) Add user

```
___ AddUser₀ _____
ΔComputer
p?:            PERSON
──────────────────
p? ∉ users
users' = users ∪ {p?}
loggedIn' = loggedIn

```

```
___ AddUserError _____
ΞComputer
p?:          PERSON
reply!:      RESPONSE
────────────────────────
p? ∈ users
reply! = AlreadyAUser
```

AddUser ≙
(AddUser$_0$ ∧ [reply!: RESPONSE | reply! = OK]) ∨ AddUserError

7.3) Remove user

```
___ RemoveUser$_0$ _____
ΔComputer
p?:          PERSON
────────────────────────
p? ∈ users
p ∉ loggedIn
users' = users \ {p?}
loggedIn' = loggedIn
```

```
___ RemoveUserError _____
ΞComputer
p?:          PERSON
reply!:      RESPONSE
────────────────────────
(p? ∉ users ∧
 reply! = NotAUser)
∨
(p? ∈ users ∧
 p? ∈ loggedIn ∧
 reply! = LoggedIn)
```

RemoveUser ≙
(RemoveUser$_0$ ∧ [reply!: RESPONSE | reply! = OK]) ∨
RemoveUserError

7.4) Log in

```
┌─ Login₀ ─────────────────
│ ΔComputer
│ p?:            PERSON
├──────────────────────────
│ p? ∈ users
│ p? ∉ loggedIn
│ loggedIn' = loggedIn ∪ {p?}
│ users' = users
└──────────────────────────
```

```
┌─ LoginError ─────────────
│ ΞComputer
│ p?:            PERSON
│ reply!:        RESPONSE
├──────────────────────────
│ (p? ∉ users
│  reply! = NotAUser)
│ ∨
│ (p? ∈ users ∧ p? ∈ loggedIn
│  reply! = LoggedIn)
└──────────────────────────
```

Login ≙
(Login₀ ∧ [reply!: RESPONSE | reply! = OK]) ∨ LoginError

7.5) Log out

```
┌─ Logout₀ ────────────────
│ ΔComputer
│ p?:            PERSON
├──────────────────────────
│ p? ∈ users
│ p? ∈ loggedIn
│ loggedIn' = loggedIn \ {p?}
│ users' = users
└──────────────────────────
```

```
┌─ LogoutError ──────────────
│ ΞComputer
│ p?:          PERSON
│ reply!:      RESPONSE
├────────────────────────────
│ (p? ∉ users
│  reply! = NotAUser)
│ ∨
│ (p? ∈ users
│  p? ∉ loggedIn
│  reply = NotLoggedIn)
└────────────────────────────
```

Logout ≙
(Logout$_0$ ∧ [reply!: RESPONSE | reply! = OK]) ∨ LogoutError

Chapter 8

8.1)

∀ p: PERSON • p ∈ loggedIn ⇒ p ∈ user

8.2)

users ≠ ∅ ⇒ ∃ p: PERSON • p ∈ user

8.3)

#users = 1 ⇒ ∃$_1$ p: PERSON • p ∈ user

8.4)

prime(n) == ¬∃ m: N | m ≠ 1 ∧ m ≠ n • divisible(n, m)

8.5)

Government ≙
Computer [POLITICIAN / PERSON,
parliament / users,
Cabinet / loggedIn]

Chapter 9

9.1)

> Latin: LANGUAGE
> Latin ∉ ran speaks

9.2)

> # speaks (| {Switzerland} |) = 4

9.3)

> EC: ℙCOUNTRY
> speaksInEC: COUNTRY ↔ LANGUAGE
>
> speaksInEC = EC ◁ speaks

9.4)

> grandParent: PERSON ↔ PERSON
> grandParent = parent ; parent

9.5)

> firstCousin: PERSON ↔ PERSON
> firstCousin = ((grandParent ; grandParent˜) \ sibling) \ id PERSON

Chapter 10

10.1) *bookedTo* is a function since for any given room at most one person can book it. A person can book any number of rooms.

10.2) The function is partial since not all rooms have been booked.

10.3) line 1: gives the schema a name
    line 2: incorporates the schema *ΔHotel*; permits reference to state variables before and after this operation.

line 3: $p?$ is an input variable – the person making the booking

line 4: $r?$ is an input variable – the room to be booked

line 5: the room must not already be booked

line 6: the maplet relating the room to the person is included in the new value of the function *bookedTo*.

10.4)

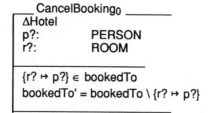

```
┌─ CancelBooking₀ ─────────
│ ΔHotel
│ p?:          PERSON
│ r?:          ROOM
├───────────────────────────
│ {r? ↦ p?} ∈ bookedTo
│ bookedTo' = bookedTo \ {r? ↦ p?}
└───────────────────────────
```

10.5) line 1: gives schema a name

line 2: incorporates the schema *ΔHotel*; permits reference to state variables before and after this operation

line 3: $p?$ is an input variable – the person making the booking

line 4: $r?$ is an input variable – the room to be booked

line 5: the room must already be booked to this person

line 6: the maplet relating the room to the person is removed from the new value of the function *bookedTo*.

Chapter 11

11.1)

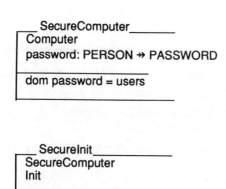

```
┌─ SecureComputer ──────────
│ Computer
│ password: PERSON ⇸ PASSWORD
├───────────────────────────
│ dom password = users
└───────────────────────────
```

11.2)

```
┌─ SecureInit ──────────────
│ SecureComputer
│ Init
├───────────────────────────
│ password = ∅
└───────────────────────────
```

11.3)

```
┌─── SecureAddUser ──────────
│ AddUser
│ ΔSecureComputer
├────────────────────────────
│ password' = password ∪ {p? ↦ dummy}
│
└────────────────────────────
```

11.4)

```
┌─── SecureLogin₀ ───────────
│ ΔSecureComputer
│ Login
│ pwd?:          PASSWORD
├────────────────────────────
│ pwd? = password p?
│ password' = password
│
└────────────────────────────
```

11.5)

```
┌─── ChangePassword₀ ────
│ ΔSecureComputer
│ p?:           PERSON
│ old?, new?:  PASSWORD
├────────────────────────────
│ p? ∈ loggedIn
│ password p? = old?
│ password' = password ⊕ {p? ↦ new?}
│
└────────────────────────────
```

Chapter 12

12.1)

u ⌢ v	= ⟨ London, Amsterdam, Madrid, Paris, Frankfurt ⟩
rev (u ⌢ v)	= ⟨ Frankfurt , Paris, Madrid, Amsterdam, London ⟩
rev u	= ⟨ Madrid, Amsterdam, London ⟩
rev v	= ⟨ Frankfurt , Paris ⟩
rev v ⌢ rev u	= ⟨ Frankfurt , Paris, Madrid, Amsterdam, London ⟩

12.2)

squash (2..4 ◁ rev (u ⌢ v)) = ⟨ Paris, Madrid, Amsterdam ⟩

12.3)

squash (4..2 ◁ rev (u ⌢ v))= ⟨ ⟩

12.4)

u ⌢ v ↾ { London, Moscow, Paris, Rome } = ⟨ London, Paris ⟩

12.5)

tail (u ⌢ v) ⌢ front ⟨ Moscow, Berlin, Warsaw ⟩
= ⟨ Amsterdam, Madrid, Paris, Frankfurt , Moscow, Berlin ⟩

Chapter 13

13.1)

[BYTE]   the set of all bytes

```
┌─ Filing ──────────────
│ file:          seq BYTE
│
└───────────────────────
```

13.2)

```
┌─ Init ────────────────
│ Filing
├───────────────────────
│ file = ⟨ ⟩
│
└───────────────────────
```

13.3)

```
┌─ Insert₀ ──────────────
│ ΔFiling
│ new?:          seq BYTE
│ after?:        N
├────────────────────────
│ after? ∈ 0 ∪ dom file
│ (∃ front, back: seq BYTE | #front = after? •
│ file = front ⌢ back
│ file' = front ⌢ new? ⌢ back)
│
└────────────────────────
```

The position must be in range. The new sequence is inserted *after* the given position.

13.4)

```
┌─ Delete₀ ─────────────────────
│ ΔFiling
│ start?:      N
│ end?:        N
├───────────────────────────────
│ start? ∈ dom file
│ end? ∈ dom file
│ start? ≤ end?
│ (∃ front, toGo, back: seq BYTE |
│  #front = start? − 1
│  #toGo = end? − start? + 1 •
│  file = front ⌢ toGo ⌢ back
│  file' = front ⌢ back)
└───────────────────────────────
```

The start- and end positions must be in range. All bytes between start- and end positions inclusive are deleted.

13.5)

```
┌─ Copy₀ ───────────────────────
│ ΞFiling
│ start?:      N
│ end?:        N
│ buffer!      seq BYTE
├───────────────────────────────
│ start? ∈ dom file
│ end? ∈ dom file
│ start? ≤ end?
│ (∃ front, back: seq BYTE |
│  #front = start? − 1
│  #buffer! = end? − start? + 1 •
│  file = front ⌢ buffer! ⌢ back)
└───────────────────────────────
```

The start- and end positions must be in range. All bytes between start- and end positions inclusive are copied into the buffer. The file remains unchanged.

Chapter 14

14.1)

Types

[APARTMENT]	the set of all apartments
[PERSON]	the set of all persons
[TIME]	the set of all time-slots

The state

```
┌─ RentApart ─────────────────────
│ apartments:  ℙ APARTMENT
│ customers:   ℙ PERSON
│ booked:      APARTMENT ⇸ TIME ⇸ PERSON
├─────────────────────────────────
│ dom booked ⊆ apartments
│ (∀ ap: APARTMENT | ap ∈ apartments •
│   ran booked ap ⊆ customers)
│
└─────────────────────────────────
```

Only apartments belonging to the company can be booked. Bookings are only made to customers who are on record.

Initial state

```
┌─ Init ───────────────────────────
│ RentApart
├─────────────────────────────────
│ apartments = ∅
│ customers = ∅
│ booked = ∅
│
└─────────────────────────────────
```

Initially there are no apartments, no customers and no bookings.

14.2)

Operations

```
┌─── NewCustomer₀ ──────────
│ ΔRentApart
│ p?:              PERSON
├───────────────────────────
│ p? ∉ customers
│ customers' = customers ∪ {p?}
│ apartments' = apartments
│ booked' = booked
└───────────────────────────
```

This is the operation to make a new customer known. The customer must not already be known. The customer becomes known.

14.3)

```
┌─── NewApartment₀ ─────────
│ ΔRentApart
│ a?:              APARTMENT
├───────────────────────────
│ a? ∉ apartments
│ apartments' = apartments ∪ {a?}
│ customers' = customers
│ booked' = booked
└───────────────────────────
```

This is the operation to make a new apartment known. The apartment must not already be owned. The apartment becomes owned.

14.4)

```
┌─── Book₀ ─────────────────
│ ΔRentApart
│ a?:              APARTMENT
│ t?:              TIME
│ p?:              PERSON
├───────────────────────────
│ a? ∈ apartments
│ p? ∈ customers
│ t? ∉ dom booked a?
│ booked' = booked ⊕ {a? ↦ booked a? ∪ {t? ↦ p?}}
│ apartments' = apartments
│ customers' = customers
└───────────────────────────
```

This is the operation to make a booking. The apartment must be owned by the company. The customer must be known. The apartment must not already be booked at the desired time. The booking is made.

14.5)

Enquiry operation

```
┌── WhichFree ───────────
│ ΞRentApart
│ t?:          TIME
│ free!:       ℙAPARTMENT
├─────────────────────────
│ free! = { a: APARTMENT |
│ a ∈ apartments ∧ t? ∉ dom booked a • a}
│
└─────────────────────────
```

This is the enquiry operation to find out which apartments are free in a given time-slot.

Index of symbols

_	6, 75	∅	12	×	69		
Δ	6, 44	{}	12, 19	↔	71		
Ξ	6, 45	ℙ	12, 15	↦	71		
'	6, 42	F	15	dom	73		
?	6, 45	F₁	16	ran	73, 105		
!	6, 45	∪	17, 18, 21	(| |)	74		
[ ]	10, 39, 64	∩	17, 19, 20	◁	76, 104		
::=	11	/	64	▷	77		
|	11, 19, 39, 62	\	18, 65	◀	77		
:	11	#	15, 101	▶	77		
==	35, 119	•	19, 62	;	41, 79		
Z	8	..	19	∘	79		
N	9	disjoint	20	id	81		
N₁	9	partition	20	~	81, 88		
+	9, 81	true	28	↠	85		
−	9	false	28	→	87		
*	9, 81	¬	28	⊕	89		
÷	9	∧	29, 43	seq	100		
mod	9	∨	29, 43	seq₁	101		
=	12, 13	⇒	30, 43	iseq	110		
≠	13	⇔	31, 44	⟨ ⟩	20, 101		
<	13	≙	39	^	103		
≤	13	∀	61	head	102		
>	13	∃	62	last	102		
≥	13	∃₁	63	tail	102		
∈	13	↾	65, 103	front	103		
∉	14	pre	65	squash	104		
⊆	16	⨟	67, 107	rev	113		
⊂	16						

See also Appendix 1 – Collected notation

Index

abbreviation definition (*see* definition, abbreviation)

Abrial, J.-R. 4

abstraction 2, 137

addition 9

and (*see* conjunction)

anti-restriction 77
   domain (*see* domain anti-restriction)
   range (*see* range anti-restriction)

application (*see* function, application)

argument 86

arrow sign 71, 85, 88

axiomatic definition (*see* definition, axiomatic)

backward composition 79

bijection (*see* function, bijective)

books 134, 137

Boole, George 28

Boolean algebra 28

brace 12

bracket 31, 87, (*see also* sequence, bracket)

calculus
   predicate (*see* predicate calculus)
   propositional (*see* propositional calculus)
   schema (*see* schema, calculus)

capacity 23

cardinality (*see* size)

Cartesian product 69

catenation (*see* concatenation)

character 5, 9

co-restriction (*see* anti-restriction)

COBOL 92

composition
   relational 78, 79
   repeated 80
   schema (*see* schema, composition)

comprehension 19

concatenation 103

conjunction 29, 41

contained in 16

convergence 85

de Morgan, Augustus 31

declaration 11, 71

decoration 42, 44, 65
   input 45
   output 45

definition
   abbreviation 35
   axiomatic 40, 74, 89

delta convention 44

Descartes 69

diacritical mark 5

difference 18

digraph (*see* directed graph)

directed graph 70

disjoint 20

disjunction 29, 32

division 9

dom (*see* domain)

domain 73, 85, 87, 89, 100, 102, 136

domain anti-restriction 77

domain restriction 76

element 8, 14

enquiry 26, 58, 137

equivalence 13, 30

161